with **Professor Grammar**

Herbert Puchta · Jeff Stranks · Peter Lewis-Jones

GRAMMAR PRACTICE

A complete grammar workout for teen students

HELBLING LANGUAGES
www.helblinglanguages.com

GRAMMAR PRACTICE 3
by Herbert Puchta, Jeff Stranks, Peter Lewis-Jones
© Helbling Languages

ISBN 978-1-107-62852-6

Design and layout by Amanda Hockin

Illustrated by Roberto Battestini, Moreno Chiacchiera, Giovanni Giorgi Pierfranceschi.

The publisher would like to thank the following for their kind permission to reproduce the following photographs:

Bloomsbury, J.K. Rowling, *Harry Potter and the Half-Blood Prince* p28; **Dreamstime** p9 (Buckingham Palace); **©iStockphoto.com** p63 (Printing press); **Library of Congress** p57 (Wilma Rudolph); **NASA** p28; **Shutterstock** p9, p24, p26, p28 (Statue of Liberty; James Cameron), 42, p50, p63 (Colin Firth), p65; **Wikimedia Commons** p28 (Titanic; Olympic flag), p57.

All rights reserved, no part of this publication may be reproduced, stored in a retrieval system, or transmitted in any form or by any means, electronic, mechanical, photocopying, recording, or otherwise, without the prior written permission of the Publishers.

Contents

Introduction	04
Present simple (revision)	05
Past simple (revision)	07
Past continuous and Past simple	11
when / before / after / during / while	15
be going to (revision)	17
The future: *be going to, will,* present continuous	19
Comparatives	20
Superlatives	22
as ... as	25
Relative pronouns	28
Personal pronouns and possessives	30
Reflexive pronouns	32
Indefinite pronouns	34
First Conditional	36
Present perfect with *for / since*	39
Past simple and Present perfect	43
Present perfect continuous	48
be allowed to	53
could / couldn't (ability)	56
be able to	58
can't be / must be	61
Present simple passive / Past simple passive	62
Second Conditional	66
Appendix	71

Introduction

Dear student,

As you know, all serious sportspeople train regularly. Regular training means better performances in all sports from swimming to running, and football to table tennis. And soon what seems like hard work miraculously becomes more and more fun!

And grammar is no different. If you train regularly you make fewer mistakes, get better results and have much more fun. The exercises in both this book and the CD-ROM have been created so that they guarantee excellent results when done consistently. Ideally you should be practising your grammar in short frequent sessions rather than last-minute intensive bouts of study before an exam or class test. How about practising for ten minutes every day? Try it out and you'll soon see positive results!

You'll get the following support in both the book and the CD-ROM:

- the Contents list allows you to easily find the topics you want to practise
- each chapter starts with a summary of the most important topics and rules
- next to the summary there is a message from Professor Grammar, your mascot throughout the book. When you see the symbol, you can go to the CD-ROM.
- in the *How it works* section on the CD-ROM, Professor Grammar will explain specific grammar structures. Then go to the *Check it out* section to double-check you have understood everything.
- at this point you can decide whether you prefer to 'train' using the CD-ROM or the book. In the CD-ROM there are two or three exercises per chapter. Once you've done each exercise you can check your results by listening to the answer (LISTEN). But remember: listening to it first will not help you!
- in the book there are one or more pages of exercises per chapter. The exercises are ordered progressively according to difficulty, from the easiest to the most challenging.
- in the Appendix there is a list of all the grammar points, with tables and rules. Plus the answer keys.
- last but not least, each chapter in the CD-ROM has a cartoon with a fun quiz. Yes, Professor Grammar has some tricks up his sleeve to make sure you have fun while you are learning!

And now, what are you waiting for … let's get started!

All the best from the team of authors,

Herbert Puchta
Jeff Stranks
Peter Lewis-Jones

Present simple (revision)

Hello! See me on the CD-ROM to discover more about *present simple (revision)* and to learn better when to use it.

You use the *present simple* to talk about what people always do. You also use it to talk about things which are always true. Remember: add –s to the 3rd person singular; use **don't / doesn't** to make the negative; and use **do / does** to make questions.

Sandra **lives** in Scotland, but Paul and Andy **live** in Ireland.
I **don't like** football, and Steve **doesn't like** basketball.
Do people in the USA eat a lot? **Does** she eat a lot?
Lots of tourists **come** to London every year.

1 Underline the correct options.

1 Mike *live / lives* in London.
2 We *play / playing* football every Saturday.
3 I *play / plays* the guitar in a band.
4 I *don't want / not want* to go to school today.
5 They *go / goes* on holiday to France every year.
6 *Do / Does* your sister go to your school?
7 Joanna *don't / doesn't* like horror films.
8 Where *do / does* you live?

2 Complete each sentence with the correct form of a verb from the box.

watch
live
think
want
go
speak
not know
not go

1 Alessandra always .... to school by bus.
2 They .... the answer to the question.
3 We .... to the cinema very often.
4 My brother never .... horror films – he's too scared!
5 .... Sandra .... French?
6 .... you .... another sandwich?
7 It's so funny. Andy .... Paris is in Italy!
8 Where .... Danny ....? In Charles Street?

3 Read the jokes. Put the verbs in brackets into the correct form of the *present simple*.

Joke 1

A man [1]........................ (go) into a pizza place. He's hungry and he [2]........................ (want) a pizza! The girl [3]........................ (say): 'Hello. Can I help you?' 'Yes, I [4]........................ (want) a pizza, please. Cheese, tomato, and mushrooms. But no onions – I [5]........................ (not like) onions, thanks.'

And then the girl [6]........................ (ask) him: '[7]........................ you .... (want) a thin pizza or a thick one?' And the man [8]........................ (say): 'Oh, a thick one, please.' 'OK,' says the girl. 'And what size? Small, medium or large?' The man [9]........................ (think) for a moment. 'Medium, please.'

'OK. And [10]........................ you .... (want) the pizza cut into four slices or six slices?' And the man [11]........................ (say): 'Oh, just four, please. I [12]........................ (not think) I can eat six slices!'

Joke 2

A man ¹³.................. (see) a sign outside a house. The sign ¹⁴.................. (say): 'Buy My Talking Dog.' The man ¹⁵.................. (knock) on the door. A woman ¹⁶.................. (show) him the dog and then she ¹⁷.................. (leave) the room.

The man asks the dog: '¹⁸.................. you really .... (talk)?' The dog says: 'Oh yes. In fact I ¹⁹.................. (speak) four languages. Sometimes the President ²⁰.................. (use) me as a spy. I sit in rooms and I listen. The people from the other countries never think that a dog can understand!'

The man ²¹.................. (run) back to the woman. 'How much do you want for the dog?'
'£20.'
'But I ²².................. (not understand)! Why only £20? That dog is fantastic!'
'Because,' the woman says, 'the dog's a liar. It ²³.................. (not speak) four languages – it only ²⁴.................. (speak) English!'

4 Use the pictures. Complete the sentences.

1 Jim / go / school / bike / bus
   Jim goes to school on his bike. He doesn't go by bus.

2 Annie / like / pizza / hamburgers
   ....

3 Steve and Janie / go to the cinema / Fridays / Saturdays
   ....

4 Maggie / watch / tennis / football
   ....

5 My friends / listen to music / dance
   ....

6 My cat / drink / milk / water
   ....

And now go to the CD-ROM and do the **Cartoon for Fun!**

Past simple (revision)

Hello! See me on the CD-ROM to discover more about *past simple (revision)* and to learn better when to use it.

When you talk about something that happened in the past (for example, when you tell a story), you can use the *past simple*. Remember: there are two kinds of verbs:

a) regular verbs: you add **-ed** to the base form to make the past

jump – jumped   wash – washed

b) irregular verbs: you have to learn and remember their past forms

go – went   find – found

To make the negative, you use **didn't** + **the base form of the verb**

I didn't see him.

1 Write R in the box if the verb is regular, I if the verb is irregular.

1 I *phoned* [R] Emily last night and we *spoke* [ ] for hours.
2 We *drove* [ ] for about three hours and then we *stopped* [ ] for lunch.
3 I *ran* [ ] all the way but I still *arrived* [ ] late.
4 I *wanted* [ ] to tell her but Kim *thought* [ ] it was a bad idea.
5 I *played* [ ] with it for about an hour and then it *broke* [ ] .
6 I *listened* [ ] to everything she said but I *understood* [ ] nothing.
7 I *watched* [ ] TV until I *fell* [ ] asleep.
8 I *looked* [ ] at the map and *saw* [ ] that we were lost.

2 Write the infinitives of the irregular verbs in **1**.

1 ......speak......   3 ....   5 ....   7 ....
2 ....   4 ....   6 ....   8 ....

3 Complete the puzzle with the past forms of the verbs and find the person.

1 make
2 continue
3 become
4 have
5 be
6 start
7 sell
8 join
9 sing
10 can
11 know
12 lose
13 win
14 go

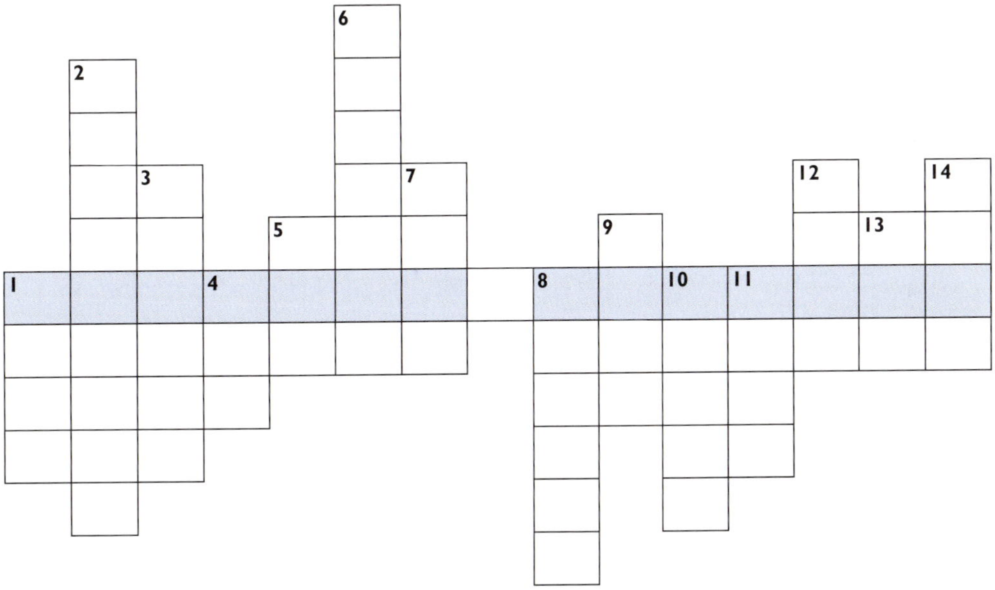

4 Complete the text with the verbs from 3.

On June 25th 2009 the music world ¹.................... one of its biggest and brightest stars. Everyone ².................... his name but few people ³.................... believe it – Michael Jackson was dead.
He ⁴.................... born on August 28th 1958 and he ⁵.................... singing in 1964 when he ⁶.................... the Jackson 5. In the group he ⁷.................... and danced with his brothers but it was clear that Michael ⁸.................... something special. In 1971 he ⁹.................... his first record as a solo singer.

He also ¹⁰.................... to sing with the Jackson 5 for several more years.
In 1982 he released his famous record, Thriller, which ¹¹.................... to number one all over the world. It ¹².................... the best-selling record ever. Michael ¹³.................... over 750 million records worldwide. He also ¹⁴.................... 15 Grammies (the Oscars of the music world).
Most people agree that at the age of 50, Michael Jackson died far too young.

5 Look at the pictures and read the sentences. Write True or False.

1 Mike didn't wash his face after breakfast. _True_
2 He left his school bag at home. ....
3 Mike ate all his lunch. ....
4 Mike didn't drink all his water. ....
5 Mike sat alone in the Maths lesson. ....
6 Mike didn't ask any questions in his Maths lesson. ....
7 Mike walked home alone. ....
8 Mike didn't remember to take his school bag. ....

6 Complete the sentences with the negative form of the verbs.

We ate onion soup but we ¹ _didn't eat_ any frog's legs.
We visited the Eiffel Tower but we ².................... .... the Louvre.

We saw Buckingham Palace but we ³.................... .... the Queen.
We rode in a London taxi but we ⁴.................... .... on a red bus.

We went up the Statue of Liberty but we ⁵.................... .... up the Empire State Building.
We took lots of photos in Central Park but we ⁶.................... .... any photos in Times Square.

We played football on the beach but we ⁷.................... .... volleyball.
We spoke lots of Portuguese but we ⁸.................... .... any Spanish.

7 Match the postcards with the correct texts in **6**. Write the numbers in the circles.

8 What did you do yesterday? Write sentences.

1 go to school .... I went to school / I didn't go to school.
2 get up before 6 a.m. ....
3 do homework ....
4 watch TV ....
5 play computer games ....
6 cook dinner ....
7 eat pizza ....
8 listen to music ....

9 Match the question and the answers.

1 Did you go to Sam's party?
2 Who did you go with?
3 What did you do?
4 Was Janice there?
5 Did you dance with her?
6 Did she talk about me?
7 Oh. What time did the party finish?
8 What time did you leave?

a Nobody. I met everyone there.
b Well, I talked and danced a lot.
c Yes, I did.
d No, she didn't.
e I don't know. I didn't stay to the end.
f Yes, I did. It was great.
g Yes, she was.
h About 9 o'clock. I had to walk Janice home.

10 Complete the dialogue.

Ben Mum, Tom called me 'stupid'.
Mum Tom, why ¹......did...... you ......call...... your brother 'stupid'?
Tom Because he broke my model.
Mum Ben, why ²...................... you .... your brother's model?
Ben Because he hit me.
Mum Tom, why ³...................... you .... your brother?
Tom Because he ate my chocolate.
Mum Ben, why ⁴...................... you .... your brother's chocolate?

Ben Because he drew on my book.
Mum Tom, why ⁵...................... you .... on your brother's book?
Tom Because he stole my pencil.
Mum Ben, why ⁶...................... you .... your brother's pencil?
Ben Because he called me 'stupid'.
Mum Tom, why ⁷...................... you .... your brother 'stupid'?
Tom Mum! We've already told you!

Read the story and put the verbs in the past tense.

The boy who cried 'wolf'

Once upon a time there ¹....was.... (be) a young boy called Timothy who ²........................ (live) in a small village by a large dark forest. His mother and father ³........................ (tell) him never to go into the forest because there were wolves there. One day, when he ⁴........................ (be) very bored, he ⁵........................ (go) into the forest. He ⁶........................ (want) some fun and ⁷........................ (decide) to play a trick on the people of the village.
"Wolf! Wolf!" he ⁸........................ (scream) at the top of his voice. "Help me. Quick. Come quickly."
All the villagers ⁹........................ (hear) his scream. They ¹⁰........................ (stop) their work, ¹¹........................ (pick) up their guns and ¹²........................ (run) into the forest. They ¹³........................ (find) Timothy but they ¹⁴........................ (not see) any wolves.
"Where ¹⁵.................. the wolves .... (go)?" ¹⁶........................ (ask) one man. But Timothy ¹⁷........................ (not answer). He just ¹⁸........................ (stand) there, laughing. Of course, the villagers ¹⁹........................ (not be) happy and that evening, Timothy's mother and father ²⁰........................ (send) him to bed without any dinner.
But the next day Timothy ²¹........................ (leave) his house and ²²........................ (go) into the forest again. He ²³........................ (think) his trick ²⁴........................ (be) so much fun. He ²⁵........................ (not care) about the villagers.
"Wolf! Wolf!" he ²⁶........................ (cry) as loud as he ²⁷........................ (can).
Again the villagers ²⁸........................ (get) their guns and ²⁹........................ (hurry) into the forest. And again they ³⁰........................ (find) Timothy laughing.
"³¹........................ you .... (think) there were wolves?" he ³²........................ (ask).
The villagers ³³........................ (be) furious. Timothy's parents ³⁴........................ (make) him say 'sorry' and promise never to do it again.
But of course, the next day, Timothy ³⁵........................ (do) it all again. He ³⁶........................ (walk) into the forest and ³⁷........................ (hide) behind a tree. But then he ³⁸........................ (see) something – eight bright yellow lights shining in the dark. Eyes! Wolves eyes!
"Wolf! Wolf!", he ³⁹........................ (shout). "Please help me! Please!"
In the village, the people ⁴⁰........................ (listen) to the boy's screams but they ⁴¹........................ (not stop) working and they ⁴²........................ (not pick) up their guns. Nobody ⁴³........................ (go) into the forest this time.
That evening Timothy ⁴⁴........................ (not come) home and after a while his parents ⁴⁵........................ (start) to get worried. Finally they ⁴⁶........................ (call) on a few neighbours and they ⁴⁷........................ (go) into the forest. They ⁴⁸........................ (look) and ⁴⁹........................ (look) everywhere but they ⁵⁰........................ (not find) Timothy. In fact, nobody ⁵¹........................ (see) the young boy ever again.

And now go to the CD-ROM and do the **Cartoon for Fun!**

Past continuous and Past simple

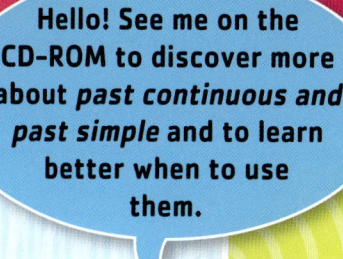

Hello! See me on the CD-ROM to discover more about *past continuous and past simple* and to learn better when to use them.

You use the *past continuous* when you talk about actions in the past that you see as going on for a longer time. You make the *past continuous* with the past simple of **be** + the **-ing** form of the verb.

> She **was sitting** at a table and she **was reading** a book.
> Last Sunday lunchtime, we **were having** lunch in a restaurant in Paris!
> I couldn't go out today because it **was raining**.

You often use the *past continuous* to talk about ongoing actions in the past which are interrupted by shorter actions. For the shorter actions, you use the *past simple*.

> I **was waiting** for my bus when I **saw** my friend Daisy.
> I **fell** off my bike while I **was riding** in the park.
> They **were taking** presents to each other's houses when they **crashed** their cars.

1 Use a verb from the box to complete each sentence.

was playing
were playing
was watching
were watching
was working
were working
was having
were having

1 I didn't hear the phone ring — I .... a shower.
2 We couldn't go to sleep last night —
   our neighbours .... music very loud.
3 Dad couldn't come to watch the match —
   he .... at my uncle's shop.
4 Sorry I didn't answer your call last night — I .... a film on TV.
5 I saw Paul ten minutes ago — he .... baseball in the park.
6 We got up really early today — at 6 o'clock we .... breakfast!
7 Steve and Jane were in the library yesterday evening —
   they .... really hard!
8 When I got to the house, my friends .... a horror film on DVD.

2 Complete each sentence. Write the verb in the correct form of the *past continuous*.

In my house, at 8 o'clock yesterday evening:

1 I .... my homework. (do)
2 My sister .... television. (watch)
3 Our two dogs .... in the kitchen. (play)
4 My grandmother .... to my mother. (talk)
5 My mother .... to my grandmother. (listen)
6 My father .... spaghetti. (cook)
7 My brother .... emails to his friends. (write)
8 Our cat .... to catch a mouse. (try)

11

3 Make the sentences negative.

1 He was working.
   He wasn't working.
2 She was listening.
   ....
3 We were enjoying our dinner.
   ....
4 It was raining.
   ....
5 You were listening to me.
   ....
6 They were speaking good English.
   ....
7 They were playing well.
   ....
8 I was looking out of the window.
   ....

4 Use the sentences from 3 to complete each sentence.

1 *It wasn't raining* .... — it was a beautiful day!
2 .... — he was playing computer games!
3 .... — they were losing 4–0 after 20 minutes!
4 .... — I was listening to the teacher!
5 .... — I couldn't understand anything at all!
6 .... — she was thinking about her boyfriend!
7 .... — you were asleep!
8 .... — the food was cold!

5 Complete the dialogue. Put the verbs in brackets into the *past continuous*.

Granddad Do you remember the day we met? Back in 1960?
Grandma Yes, I do. I remember it very well.
Granddad We met in a café.
Grandma No, we met in the park.
Granddad That's right! The park! The sun 1.................................... (shine).
Grandma No, the sun 2.................................... (not shine). It 3.................................... (rain).
Granddad Ah yes! The rain! And you 4.................................... (ride) your bike.
Grandma No, I 5.................................... (not ride) my bike. I 6.................................... (walk).
Granddad Of course — you 7.................................... (walk). And you 8.................................... (wear) a blue jacket.
Grandma No, I wasn't. I 9.................................... (wear) a brown raincoat.
Granddad Yes, I remember everything. Just like it was yesterday.
Grandma Hmm. And what 10.................................... you .... (do)?
Granddad Me? I 11.................................... (play) football with my friend Stevie Jones.
Grandma That's right. Stevie Jones. He was so good-looking.
Granddad He was. But you married me. Remember?
Grandma Yes, I remember! I 12.................................... (not wear) my glasses that day. Oh well. Everyone can make a mistake!

12

6 Find words in the puzzle to complete the sentences.

T	O	L	T	R	Y	I	N	G	A
L	A	D	A	V	I	O	P	O	W
B	R	O	K	E	W	E	N	T	A
R	R	O	I	F	I	E	N	A	I
O	I	E	N	F	O	U	N	D	T
K	V	N	G	O	I	N	G	R	I
A	E	S	D	E	Z	I	P	A	N
D	D	A	N	C	I	N	G	C	G

1 I .... my arm while I was playing football.
2 When my friends .... , I was still doing my homework.
3 I was talking to Anna when she suddenly .... very angry.
4 My dad .... to sleep while he was watching a film on TV.
5 We were .... to the cinema when my friend suddenly got ill.
6 When you phoned, I was .... to finish my homework.
7 We were .... at the party when the lights went out!
8 I was .... photographs when my camera broke.
9 While I was .... for Alex, I got a message from him.
10 He was eating a salad when he .... an insect in it!

7 Underline the correct options.

1 While I *was working* / *worked* in my bedroom, I *was hearing* / *heard* a noise outside.
2 He *was hurting* / *hurt* his hand while he *was carrying* / *carried* some heavy bags.
3 While we *were walking* / *walked* home, it *was starting* / *started* to snow.
4 When I *was getting* / *got* to Jim's house, everyone *was dancing* / *danced*.
5 A man *was shouting* / *shouted* at me while I *was running* / *ran* in the park.
6 While the teacher *was explaining* / *explained* the grammar, Mike *was falling* / *fell* asleep.
7 Someone *was knocking* / *knocked* on our door while we *were watching* / *watched* the film.
8 I *was walking* / *walked* into our house when I *was falling* / *fell* over the cat.

8 Put the verbs in brackets into the correct form: *past simple* or *past continuous*.

A Hello Jim. I ¹ *didn't see* (not see) you at school yesterday.
B That's right. I ² .... (not go) to school.
A Why not?
B Well, in the morning, while I ³ .... (have) breakfast, I suddenly ⁴ .... (feel) really ill. I ⁵ .... (have) a bad stomach ache.
A Oh dear. What ⁶ .... (happen) then?
B Well, I ⁷ .... (go) back to my bedroom. And while I ⁸ .... (sit) on my bed, I got worse. So my mum ⁹ .... (phone) for an ambulance.
A No way! An ambulance?
B Yes. But, while they ¹⁰ .... (take) me to hospital, the ambulance ¹¹ .... (crash).

A What?!
B That's right. Nobody was hurt, but we had to wait for another ambulance. And while we ¹² .... (wait), my stomach ache ¹³ .... (stop).
A You're kidding.
B No, it's true. So I ¹⁴ .... (walk) back home and I ¹⁵ .... (start) to get ready for school. But while I ¹⁶ .... (get) dressed, I ¹⁷ .... (look) at the clock.
A And?
B And it was already 10 o'clock – so I ¹⁸ .... (decide) to stay at home anyway!

9 Make the sentences. Use the verbs.

1 I / ride / when / fall off
   I was riding my bike when I fell off.
2 Garth / cook / when / hurt / hand
   ....
   ....
3 Someone / knock / window / while / Emma / watch / TV
   ....
   ....
4 Anne's phone / ring / while / do / homework
   ....
   ....
5 Karl / walk / in the woods / when / feel / something on his head
   ....
   ....

And now go to the CD-ROM and do the **Cartoon for Fun!**

when / before / after / during / while

Hello! See me on the CD-ROM to discover more about **when / before / after / during / while** and to learn better when to use them.

You use **when**, **before**, **after**, **while** to introduce time phrases.

When we got to London, we went straight to the hotel.
Before we went out for dinner, we all took a shower.
After we went to The Tower of London, we decided to have lunch.

Notice the difference between **while** and **during**. **While** is followed by a verb phrase (a structure with a verb), and **during** is followed by a noun phrase (a structure with a noun).

While we were leaving the island, the weather suddenly changed.
During our trip, we ran out of gas.

1 Match the sentences and the pictures.

☐ I broke the glass while I was doing the washing-up.
☐ I broke the glass before doing the washing-up.
☐ I broke the glass after doing the washing-up.

☐ She smiled at me before she opened my present.
☐ She smiled at me after she opened my present.
☐ She smiled at me while she was opening my present.

☐ It started raining before we had our picnic.
☐ It started raining while we were having our picnic.
☐ It started raining after we had our picnic.

2 Match the sentence halves.

A trip to the cinema.

1. Before I left my house I checked
2. When I arrived at the cinema I bought
3. After I bought my ticket I got some
4. While I was getting to my seat I spilled
5. After he stopped shouting I said
6. During the film my mobile phone
7. While I was talking on the phone the man
8. After he stopped shouting this time I threw

a popcorn and a drink and went to see the film.
b 'sorry' and sat down. Where was Jim?
c rang. It was Jim. He was in another film.
d for my phone. I needed to phone Jim at the cinema.
e next to me started shouting again.
f my ticket. I phoned Jim but he didn't answer.
g my drink on the man next to me. He wasn't happy.
h my popcorn over him and went to find Jim.

3 Underline the correct word.

1. The plane took off *while / during* a heavy storm.
2. You have to kill the monster *before / after* you can go to the next level in this game.
3. *When / Before* the lights went out, it was really dark.
4. I was having dinner *while / when* I started feeling ill.
5. *While / During* I was walking to school, I found £5 on the pavement.
6. I fell over twice *during / when* the match.
7. Mum says I have to come straight home *before / after* school.
8. *When / After* you see Lucy, can you give her this, please?

4 Read the story and choose the correct options.

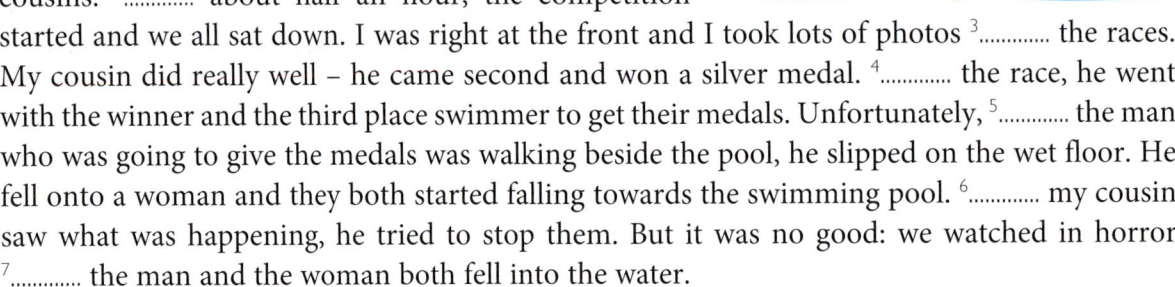

Last week I went to see one of my cousins swim in a big competition in London. We arrived early and I had lots of time ¹............ the races to talk with all my other cousins. ²............ about half an hour, the competition started and we all sat down. I was right at the front and I took lots of photos ³............ the races. My cousin did really well – he came second and won a silver medal. ⁴............ the race, he went with the winner and the third place swimmer to get their medals. Unfortunately, ⁵............ the man who was going to give the medals was walking beside the pool, he slipped on the wet floor. He fell onto a woman and they both started falling towards the swimming pool. ⁶............ my cousin saw what was happening, he tried to stop them. But it was no good: we watched in horror ⁷............ the man and the woman both fell into the water.
The man and woman were helped out of the pool and everybody laughed and clapped. And ⁸............ about three minutes, the man and woman started laughing too!

1 a) while   b) before   c) after
2 a) After   b) Before   c) When
3 a) while   b) during   c) before
4 a) During   b) While   c) After
5 a) while   b) during   c) after
6 a) While   b) When   c) Before
7 a) during   b) before   c) while
8 a) after   b) before   c) while

And now go to the CD-ROM and do the **Cartoon for Fun!**

be going to (revision)

You use **be going to** when you want to talk about future plans or intentions. You also use **be going to** to say that you think something is almost sure to happen in the future.

I**'m going to stay** in bed until 11.00 tomorrow morning!
We **aren't going to visit** our grandparents tomorrow – they're away on holiday.
Look at all those clouds – it**'s going to rain**.
It **isn't going to be** easy to get a job when I leave school.

Hello! See me on the CD-ROM to discover more about *be going to (revision)* and to learn better when to use it.

1 Match the sentences / questions with the pictures.

 a
 b
 c
 d
 e
 f
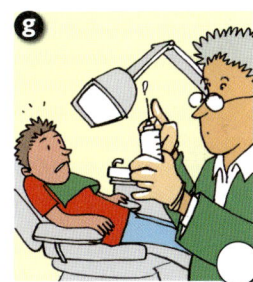 g
 h
 i
 j

1 OK – what are we going to do now?
2 Where are you going to keep it?
3 He's going to hurt himself.
4 Oh dear – I think this is going to hurt!
5 I don't think we are going to finish our game.
6 I'm going to take a break.
7 This is going to be really good fun!
8 I'm going to be late for school.
9 He's going to take us for a walk.
10 Dad isn't going to be very happy.

2 Complete the mini-dialogues. Use the correct form of *be going to*.

1 **A** We're going for a walk. ....*Are*........ you ....*going to*........ come with us?
   B No, thanks. I .... stay here and watch TV.
2 **A** I think it .... rain this afternoon.
   B Really? The newspaper says it .... be warm and sunny.
3 **A** What .... you .... cook tonight?
   B Nothing – we .... have dinner in that new Italian restaurant.
4 **A** Next week I .... watch a really famous band play in a concert.
   B Really? Who .... see? Tell me!

17

5 A What .... you .... get for your birthday?

B I'm not sure — but I think my parents .... give me a new mobile phone.

6 A .... you .... watch the match tonight?

B No, I .... study. There's a test tomorrow, remember?

3 Complete the dialogue. Put the items in brackets into present simple or a form of *be going to*.

Hannah Bye, Sally. See you in September!

Sally September? What? Where are you going?

Hannah Madrid. (I / spend) ¹ *I'm going to spend* the next two months in Spain.

Sally Two months? In Spain? What (you / do) ² *are you going to do* in Spain?

Hannah Lots of things. (I / love) ³.................... languages, so (I / take) ⁴.................... Spanish lessons.

Sally But — (you / speak) ⁵.................... Spanish already?

Hannah No! Well, (I / speak) ⁶.................... a little, but I want to be much, much better. In Madrid, (I / practise) ⁷.................... every day! When I come back in September, (my Spanish / be) ⁸.................... perfect!

Sally Where (you / stay) ⁹....................?

Hannah Oh, my mother's got an old friend from school, Jean — (she / live) ¹⁰.................... in Madrid, so (I / stay) ¹¹.................... in her flat.

Sally Oh, Hannah. So (I / not see) ¹².................... you for two months! (you / miss) ¹³.................... me?

Hannah Of course! But don't worry! (You / have) ¹⁴.................... a really good time this summer, too — I'm sure of it!

4 Write sentences that are true for you.

1 Tomorrow …

  a I ....

  b the weather ....

2 Next week …

  a I ....

  b my best friend ....

3 Next year …

  a I ....

  b my family ....

And now go to the CD-ROM and do the **Cartoon for Fun!**

The future: *be going to*, *will*, present continuous

To talk about the future, we can use:
be going to (plans and intentions)
will / won't (predictions, sudden decisions, promises)
the present continuous (plans and arrangements already made)

I**'m going to** study hard.
It **will be** cold tomorrow.
We**'re spending** Christmas at home.

1 Match the sentences to the pictures to tell the story of Sleeping Beauty.

I'm going to give her a kiss.

Next week we're having a big celebration for the birth of our daughter. Please come.

Your wish will come true. Next year you will have a daughter.

When she is fifteen years old, the Princess will prick herself with a spindle and will fall down dead!

We're going to invite the fairies to a big party.

The princess will not die. She will fall into a deep sleep that will last one hundred years.

Come and celebrate with us. We're getting married next month.

I am not afraid. I'm going to find Sleeping Beauty.

1 ....

2 ....

3 ....

4 ....

5 ....

6 ....
A hundred years later

7 ....

8 ....

Comparatives

Hello! See me on the CD-ROM to discover more about *comparatives* and to learn better when to use them.

You make the comparative form of all one-syllable adjectives, and some two-syllable adjectives, by adding **-er** to the adjective. You make the comparative form of all other two-syllable adjectives, and adjectives with three or four syllables, by using **more** + **adjective**.

Be careful with spelling: **y** at the end of an adjective becomes **i**; and sometimes the final letter is doubled (**big – bigger**; **hot – hotter** etc).
Irregular adjectives: **good → better** / **bad → worse**

My sister's **taller than** me.
I'm **happier** today **than** I was yesterday.
His new film is **better than** his last one.

1 Read the sentences. Tick the correct picture for each sentence.

1 The watch is cheaper than the ring.

2 The grey dog is faster than the white one.

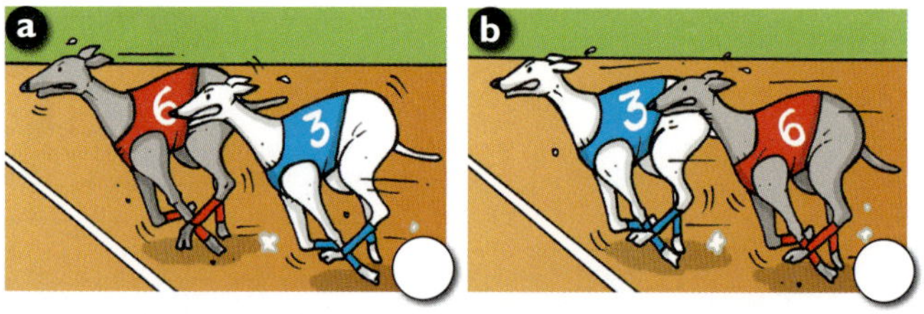

3 The black cat is heavier than the white one.

4 The book was more interesting than the film.

5 The Reds are better than the Blues.

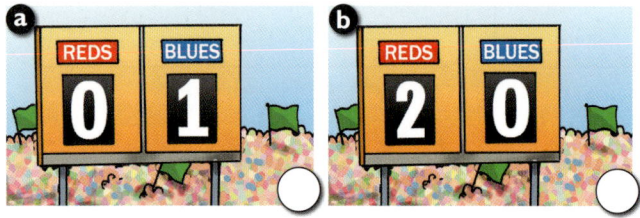

6 The Grand Hotel is worse than the Palace Hotel.

2 Underline the correct options.

1 This book is really <u>interesting</u> / more interesting.
2 My friend's new mobile phone is good / better than his old one.
3 Mmm! This food tastes good / more good.
4 This film is very scary / more scary!
5 It's warm / warmer today than it was yesterday.
6 I think your hair is nice / nicer than mine.
7 It's raining again! It's a horrible / more horrible day today!
8 Patsy is always good at tests. No one in our class is intelligent / more intelligent than her.

3 Complete the sentences using the adjective from the first part of the sentence in the comparative form.

1 Todd's nice, but Harry's .... *nicer* ....
2 This snake is dangerous, but that snake is ....
3 My Internet is fast, but yours is ....
4 The old game was difficult, but the new one is ....
5 'Pizza Quick' is good, but 'Super Pizza' is ....
6 Your dad's car is bad, but my dad's car is .... !
7 The first question was easy, and the second question was .... !
8 I thought the programme was interesting, but the other one was ....

4 Complete the texts. Use the correct form of the words in brackets.

Soapo!

It's ¹............... (good) than your old shampoo! And it's ²............... (cheap) and ³............... (economical) than your usual shampoo, too!

Get your clothes ⁴............... (clean) than ever before!

Use Soapo!!

What's the matter?

Do you need a ⁵............... (fast) Internet connection than the one you've got now?

Call us at Speedynet

We've got services that are ⁶............... (quick) and ⁷............... (powerful) than you can imagine!

For a ⁸............... (good) Internet connection than your present one – call **Speedynet** now!

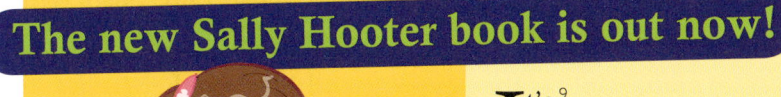

The new Sally Hooter book is out now!

It's ⁹............... (exciting), ¹⁰............... (funny) and ¹¹............... (frightening) than all the other books put together! Perhaps you think it's ¹²............... (expensive) than the other books? Well, you're wrong! We've taken £2.50 off – call now for your copy!

And now go to the CD-ROM and do the **Cartoon for Fun!**

Superlatives

Hello! See me on the CD-ROM to discover more about *superlatives* and to learn better when to use them.

You use the superlative form of adjectives when you compare one person or thing in a group with two or more other people or things in the same group. You make superlatives by using **the** + **adjective** + **-est** for one-syllable or some two-syllable adjectives (**the biggest** / **the fastest** / **the cleverest** etc). For all other two-syllable adjectives, and adjectives with three or more syllables, you use **the most** + **adjective** (**the most interesting** etc). Again, be careful with spelling.

I'm **the** tall**est** in the class.
It's **the** big**gest** ship in the world.
It's **the** prett**iest** cat in the shop.

1 Look at the pictures and tick (✓) the correct option.

 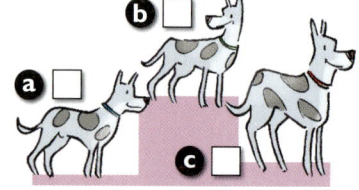 

1 The fattest dog.   2 The tallest dog.   3 The scariest dog.

4 The most expensive dog.   5 The biggest dog.   6 The shortest dog.

2 Look at the underlined words. Write **A** for adjective, **C** for comparative or **S** for superlative.

The weather man says that tomorrow is going to be ¹the coldest day of the year. But it can't be any ²colder than it is today. It's ³freezing . If you're going out Hannah, wear ⁴the warmest clothes you've got. If you don't believe me look at your ⁵younger brother. He's just come in with ⁶the reddest cheeks I've ever seen. He got straight into a ⁷hot bath to try and get a bit ⁸warmer . I think he's still there. In fact, why don't you stay at home? It's the ⁹best place to be on a day like this. It's definitely ¹⁰smarter than going shopping with your friends. You'll only spend all your money on ¹¹expensive clothes and things you don't really need. I'll make you the ¹²best soup you've ever tasted and then we can all sit together and watch a ¹³romantic film on TV. Now isn't that a ¹⁴better idea than going out? What do you think Hannah? Hannah …?

3 Underline the superlatives and then write your answers.

1 The most interesting book I've read – ....
2 My best friends – ....
3 The funniest person I know – ....
4 The oldest person I know – ....
5 The most amazing place I've visited – ....
6 The scariest film I've seen – ....
7 My most expensive thing I have – ....
8 The worst day of the week – ....

4 Write the superlative form of each adjective in the table.

~~old~~   young   hot   good   funny   interesting   bad   scary
fat   amazing   ugly   red   tall   exciting   pretty

the small**est**	the big**g**est	the heav**iest**	the **most** beautiful	irregular
oldest				

5 Complete with the superlative forms.

WELCOME TO
THE WORLD'S ¹.................................. (GREAT) SHOW!

Come and see some of
².................................. (incredible) animals on the planet:

The world's ³............ (fat) frog – You won't believe your eyes.

The world's ⁴............ (old) tortoise – It's 150 years old.

Watch the fantastic WALDO.
His magic tricks are
⁵.................................. (amazing) in the country.

And, of course, we have
⁶.................................. (funny) clown in the world.

DON'T MISS THE FUN. IT'S ⁷.................. (GOOD) NIGHT OUT IN TOWN.

23

6 Complete the sentences with the superlatives.

1 It was .... day of my life. (long)
2 It was .... thing I've seen. (silly)
3 It was .... joke I've heard. (funny)
4 It was .... film I've seen. (scary)
5 It was .... day of my life. (happy)
6 It was .... day of my life. (bad)
7 It was .... problem we faced. (big)
8 It was .... meal I've had for a long time. (good)

7 Match these sentences with the sentences from **6** that come before them.

I couldn't stop laughing. ☐
I've never worked so hard. [1]
The day I married my beautiful wife. ☐
The day I crashed my dad's car. ☐

What a great restaurant. ☐
A dog wearing jeans and a leather jacket. ☐
I couldn't watch most of it. ☐
We only had sea water to drink. ☐

8 Use the adjectives in the correct form to complete the sentences.

fast
expensive
small
tall
rich
big
long
heavy

World Record Breakers

1 .... sandcastle in the world was 9.6 m high (31 ft 6 in).
2 Xie Qiuping of China has .... hair in the world. It is 5.627 m long.
3 .... apple was from Japan. It weighed 1.849 kg.
4 .... time for running 100 m with no shoes on ice is 17.35 seconds.
5 .... mobile phone in the world is worth 850,000 pounds.
6 .... football club in 2007 was Real Madrid, from Spain, with more than 270 million pounds.
7 .... box of chocolates in the world had 20,000 chocolates in it.
8 .... newspaper in the world is 32 × 22 mm.

And now go to the CD-ROM and do the *Cartoon for Fun!*

as ... as

Hello! See me on the CD-ROM to discover more about *as ... as* and to learn better when to use them.

You use **(not) as ... as** + **adjective** to say that two people or things are the same or not the same.

I'm **as** clever **as** you = We're the same in intelligence.
I'm **not as** clever **as** you. = You're cleverer than me.
The film is **as** good **as** the book. = They are the same – both are good.
The film is **not as** good **as** the book. = The book is better.

1 Read the sentences and tick Reg's things.

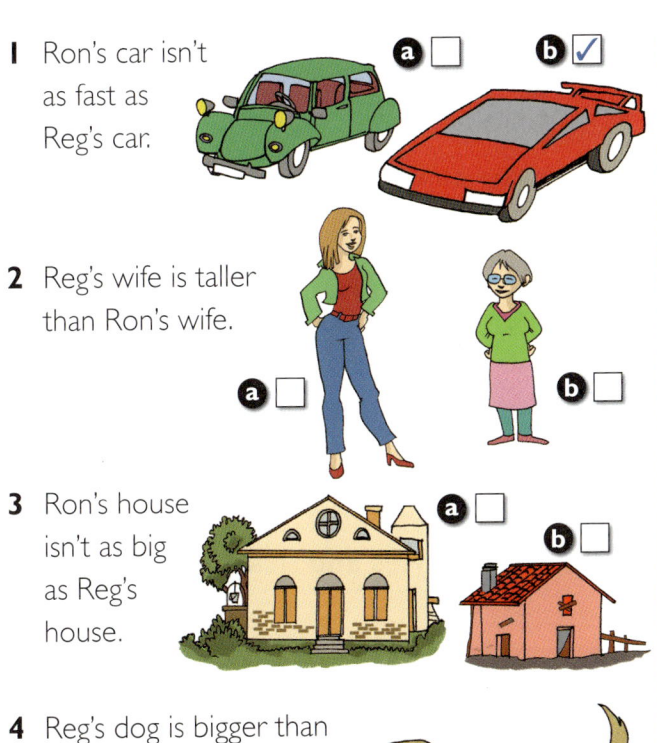

1 Ron's car isn't as fast as Reg's car.   a ☐ b ✓
2 Reg's wife is taller than Ron's wife.   a ☐ b ☐
3 Ron's house isn't as big as Reg's house.   a ☐ b ☐
4 Reg's dog is bigger than Ron's dog.   a ☐ b ☐
5 Ron's pool is smaller than Reg's pool.   a ☐ b ☐
6 Ron's bike is slower than Reg's bike.   a ☐ b ☐
7 Reg's bank account is bigger than Ron's bank account.   a ☐ b ☐
8 Ron's smile isn't as big as Reg's smile.   a ☐ b ☐

2 Look back at 1 and decide if the sentences are True or False.

1 Reg's car isn't as modern as Ron's car.   ....
2 Ron's wife is older than Reg's wife.   ....
3 Ron's house isn't as expensive as Reg's house.   ....
4 Ron's dog isn't as dangerous as Reg's dog.   ....
5 Reg's pool isn't as deep as Ron's pool.   ....
6 Ron's bike is more expensive than Reg's bike.   ....
7 Reg isn't as rich as Ron.   ....
8 Ron is happier than Reg.   ....

3 Match the expressions that mean the same.

1 cheaper
2 slower
3 shorter
4 smaller
5 more dangerous
6 heavier
7 more difficult
8 uglier

a not as fast as
b not as safe as
c not as light as
d not as tall as
e not as pretty as
f not as easy as
g not as expensive as
h not as big as

4 Complete the popular expressions with the words in the box.

night   mouse
ice   wolf
ABC   houses

1 as *cold* as ....
2 as *hungry* as a ....
3 as *quiet* as a ....
4 as *safe* as ....
5 as *easy* as ....
6 as *black* as ....

5 Use the words in italics from 4 to complete the sentences.

1 Can I have more potatoes mum? I'm ....
2 Don't worry about your dog. He'll be .... with me.
3 It was so dark in the cave. It was ....
4 Your hands are freezing. They're ....
5 The test was .... I think I've done really well.
6 I didn't hear her come into the room. She was ....

6 Look at the information in the table. Read the sentences and tick T (True) or F (False).

	A	B	C
size	3 bedrooms	10 bedrooms	3 bedrooms
year	1735	1875	1980
price	£500,000	£5 million	£225,000

     T F
1 House A is more expensive than house C. ☐ ☐
2 House A is as big as house C. ☐ ☐
3 House B isn't as new as house A. ☐ ☐
4 House B isn't as expensive as house A. ☐ ☐
5 House B is bigger than house C. ☐ ☐

     T F
6 House C is older than house B. ☐ ☐
7 House A is the oldest. ☐ ☐
8 House B is the biggest. ☐ ☐
9 House C is the most expensive. ☐ ☐

7 Correct the false sentences in 6.

☐ ....
☐ ....
☐ ....
☐ ....

8 Complete the text using the comparative, superlative or as … as form of the adjectives in brackets.

I love ice hockey! It's ¹.................................... (good) sport in the world. OK, so it's ².................................... (not popular) football or rugby in this country but it's much ³.................................... (exciting) than any of them. People say it's too dangerous but it's ⁴.................................... (not dangerous) football, for example. Many more people hurt themselves playing football. It's such a quick game. It's ⁵.................................... (fast) game I've ever played. You can't rest for a second. I play for a kid's team in my home city of Manchester. We're not great. In fact we're one of ⁶.................................... (bad) teams in the country but at least we're ⁷.................................... (not bad) Liverpool. They're ⁸.................................... (terrible) team I've ever played against. I'm quite small. I'm ⁹.................................... (small) player on our team but my trainer says I'm ¹⁰.................................... (good) most of the other players. When I get ¹¹.................................... (big) I'm going to be ¹².................................... (great) player in the country and win a gold medal for the UK at the Winter Olympics!

9 Rewrite the sentences so they mean the same.

Example: Paul is taller than Steve. *Steve is not as tall as Paul.*

1 The weather was worse in July than it was in January.
....
2 London is dirtier than Manchester. ....
3 This kids' pool is warmer than the adult pool. ....
4 Thrillers are more exciting than love stories. ....
5 Dave is funnier than Joshua. ....
6 Maths is easier than Science. ....
7 Squash is more difficult than tennis. ....
8 Our dog is friendlier than our cat. ....

And now go to the CD-ROM and do the Cartoon for Fun!

Relative pronouns

Hello! See me on the CD-ROM to discover more about *relative pronouns* and to learn better when to use them.

You use relative pronouns (**who** / **that** / **which**) to add extra information about the person or thing you are talking about. You use **who** or **that** to refer to people. You use **that** or **which** to refer to things.

He's the guy **who** / **that** bought my father's old car.

I've got a dog **that** / **which** chases cats all the time.

There were three questions **that** / **which** were very difficult for everyone.

 1 Write or in the spaces to complete the questions. Then tick what you think the answers are!

1 What is the name of the statue .... stands in New York?
   a ☐ Statue of Freedom
   b ☐ Statue of Liberty
   c ☐ Statue of Liberation

2 What is the name of the canal .... joins the Atlantic Ocean and the Pacific Ocean?
   a ☐ Suez Canal
   b ☐ English Channel
   c ☐ Panama Canal

3 What is the name of the city .... hosted the Olympic Games in 2008?
   a ☐ Beijing
   b ☐ London
   c ☐ Athens

4 What is the name of the first satellite .... went into space in 1957?
   a ☐ Apollo
   b ☐ Robot
   c ☐ Sputnik

5 What is the name of the person .... made the films *Avatar* and *Titanic*?
   a ☐ James Cameron
   b ☐ John Carson
   c ☐ Johnny Cash

6 What is the name of the player .... scored the winning goal in the 2010 World Cup final?
   a ☐ Torres
   b ☐ Iniesta
   c ☐ Messi

7 What is the name of the woman .... wrote the Harry Potter stories?
   a ☐ R. K. Jowling
   b ☐ R. J. Cowling
   c ☐ J. K. Rowling

8 What is the name of the machine .... John Logie Baird invented in 1925?
   a ☐ The telephone
   b ☐ The television
   c ☐ The computer

2 Cross out the word that cannot be used.

1 The park is the place ~~who~~ / which / that I like going to best.
2 She's the woman who / which / that bought my dad's old car.
3 The Danube is the river who / which / that goes through Vienna and Budapest.
4 Usain Bolt is the man who / which / that ran the fastest 100 metres in 2008.
5 The bus who / which / that goes past my house is the number 23.
6 That's the car who / which / that was in the last 'James Bond' film.
7 I really don't like people who / which / that talk too loudly.
8 What's the name of the singer who / which / that recorded this song?

3 Join the sentences. Use *who* or *which*.

1 Do you know the girl? She is talking to Tom.   *Do you know the girl who is talking to Tom?*
2 I got on a train. It was full of people. ....
3 I met a woman. She was lost. ....
4 I bought a book. It helps you learn English grammar. ....
5 My brother's got a motorbike. It goes really fast. ....
6 I don't like the boy. He sits next to me in class. ....
7 Picasso was a painter. He painted a lot of famous pictures. ....
8 That's the computer. I'm going to buy it. ....

4 Complete the text. Write one word in each space.

A bank in town was robbed yesterday. The man ¹............... robbed the bank had a gun and he was wearing a mask ²............... made him look like Donald Duck. He was working together with another man ³............... waited outside in the getaway car, a red BMW.
The people ⁴............... were in the bank were told to lie down on the floor. The woman at the bank ⁵............... gave him the money said she had never been so scared in her life. She put all the money ⁶............... was in the safe into a large, black bag. The robber took the bag and ran out of the bank. He then jumped into the car ⁷............... was waiting for him. However, the man ⁸............... was driving the getaway car made a mistake. There were some traffic lights near the bank ⁹............... were red, but the driver didn't stop. The BMW hit another car ¹⁰............... was crossing in front of it. Two policemen ¹¹............... were in the area heard the crash and arrested the two men.

And now go to the CD-ROM and do the **Cartoon for Fun!**

Personal pronouns and possessives

> Hello! See me on the CD-ROM to discover more about *personal pronouns and possessives* and to learn better when to use them.

You use pronouns to replace nouns. Instead of the **car** you can say **it** – 'it' is a pronoun. Pronouns have different forms.

Subject pronouns:

He works in a bank.
She likes rock music a lot.
They used to live in that house.

Object pronouns (after a verb or a preposition):

Most people don't like **him** very much – so they don't talk to **him**.
I phoned **her** but she didn't pick up the phone – so I didn't talk to **her**.
I saw **them** but I didn't get a chance to talk to **them**.

Possessive pronouns:

Hey – that mobile phone isn't **yours**! It's **mine**!
See that car? It used to be **ours**!
Give it back to your sister – it's **hers**.

You can also use **possessive adjectives** to talk about who something belongs to:

Hey – that's **my** phone!
This is **our** house.
Well, it's **your** decision, not mine.

1 Complete the table.

Subject pronoun	Object pronoun	Possessive adjective	Possessive pronoun
I	me	.... (bed)	....
You (*singular*)	....	your (bed)	....
He	....	his (bed)	....
She	....	.... (bed)	....
It	it	.... (bed)	....
We	....	.... (bed)	ours
You (*plural*)	....	.... (bed)	....
They	....	.... (bed)	theirs

2 Underline the correct options.

1 We haven't got any animals at home — we don't like *they* / *them* / *it*.
2 I've got a tarantula — I keep *it* / *them* / *its* in a cage.
3 Mr Hopkins is a good teacher — we really like *he* / *him* / *it*.
4 Excuse me — is this *you* / *your* / *yours* hat?
5 My brother and I think the guy in that shop doesn't like *us* / *we* / *our*.
6 My mum's really good at Maths — let's ask *she* / *hers* / *her*.
7 Paul's asked me to go with *he* / *him* / *his* to the club tonight!
8 Can you take those snakes away, please? I'm really scared of *them* / *they* / *their*.

3 Underline the correct option.

1 I'm not worried. It's not <u>my</u> / mine problem.
2 This isn't my pen. It's her / hers.
3 I think these CDs are our / ours, but I'm not sure.
4 Excuse me, waiter. This pizza isn't ours. I think it's their / theirs.
5 See that building over there? That's our / ours school.
6 Their / Theirs house is really enormous.
7 This is my chair! That chair over there is your / yours.
8 I don't like her / hers shoes very much.

4 Complete the sentences with the missing pronouns.

1 'I'm not sure, but it might be ......<u>his</u>...... .'
2 'Hey! Come back with that bicycle! It's .... !'
3 'Er, John – don't eat that pizza! I think it could be .... !'
4 'Mister – can we have that ball back, please? It's ....'
5 'Darling – are you sure that coat is .... ?'
6 'Well, they seem to think that the seats are .... , don't they?'

5 Write the correct word in each space.

1 **A** 'Sam and I are going out tonight. We're going to the cinema. Do you want to come with ¹............ ?'
   B 'Sorry, no. My aunt is coming round tonight. ²............'s had some problems recently so we really want to see ³............ . We're important to ⁴............ too, and she needs ⁵............ help.'

2 **A** Where are my glasses? I put ⁶............ on the table a few minutes ago but ⁷............ aren't there any more.
   B Perhaps dad's got them. You know, ⁸............ glasses look just like ⁹............ – so perhaps ¹⁰............ took ¹¹............ glasses by mistake?

3 **A** My sister and I are very different. ¹²............'s a lot more fun than ¹³............ .
   B Really? That's just like my brother and me. ¹⁴............ makes jokes all the time, so everyone invites ¹⁵............ to parties and things. But ¹⁶............'m much quieter. Well, it's OK – I get invited to parties sometimes too! In fact, the new girl in class invited ¹⁷............ to ¹⁸............ party next Saturday. I think she likes ¹⁹............ !

And now go to the CD-ROM and do the Cartoon for Fun!

Reflexive pronouns

> Hello! See me on the CD-ROM to discover more about *reflexive pronouns* and to learn better when to use them.

When the subject and the object of a verb are the same person, you use a reflexive pronoun as the object of the verb.

My father had an accident but he didn't hurt **himself**.
They can look after **themselves**.
So, kids – did **you** enjoy **yourselves** in London?

You can also use reflexive pronouns to emphasise that it really was the subject of the verb who did the action, without other people's help.

My little sister painted this picture **herself**.
No one wanted to help us so **we** did it **ourselves**.
My parents weren't home, so **I** cooked dinner **myself**.

1 Complete the table of reflexive pronouns. Use the example sentences above to help you.

Singular		Plural	
I	1	We	6 ....
You	2 *yourself*	You	7 ....
He	3	They	8 ....
She	4		
It	5		

2 Read the sentences. Look at the reflexive pronoun (underlined). Is it like the examples in 1 in the grammar box, or the examples in 2? Write 1 or 2 in the boxes.

1 We're going to enjoy <u>ourselves</u> tonight! [1]
2 I can't help you – you'll have to do it <u>yourself</u>. [2]
3 Be careful – don't hurt <u>yourself</u>! ☐
4 Cats are great pets because they can look after <u>themselves</u>. ☐
5 My teacher doesn't believe that I did the homework <u>myself</u>. ☐
6 I don't like looking at <u>myself</u> in the mirror. ☐
7 I couldn't go to the shop for Tom, so he went there <u>himself</u>. ☐
8 The painter was very expensive, so we decided to paint the house <u>ourselves</u>. ☐

3 Choose a phrase from the box to complete each sentence.

- hurt themselves
- ~~enjoy himself~~
- look after herself
- behaves itself
- hurt yourself
- enjoy myself
- look after yourself
- behave yourselves

1 Dad came with us to the zoo, but I think he didn't *enjoy himself* very much.
2 I heard about your accident – I hope you didn't .... too much.
3 'Tom! Susie! Stop making all this noise. Sit quietly and ....!'
4 When cats fall, they often don't .... at all. They're amazing.
5 I'm looking forward to the party tonight – I think I'm going to .... a lot!
6 We've trained our dog well – it doesn't bark or run around much. It .... nearly all the time.
7 'Bye, Graham! It was great to see you here! Have a good trip and ....!'
8 My baby sister's four now, but of course she still can't .... at all.

4 Match the beginnings and endings. Draw lines.

1 I hope you didn't
2 It's a great book. I'm surprised that she
3 No one's going to write this email for me. I guess I'll have to
4 John always looks unhappy. I don't think he ever
5 My mother fell down the stairs yesterday. She really
6 It's great you're going to New York. I'm sure you'll
7 Don't worry about my brother. He can
8 He's crazy about his appearance! He's always

a look after himself.
b enjoy yourselves.
c hurt yourself.
d looking at himself.
e enjoys himself.
f hurt herself.
g write it myself.
h wrote it herself.

5 Write the correct reflexive pronoun in each space.

What a day again today! Class 3B really are a problem. I've asked the head teacher to do something about them but I think he's afraid of them, so I'm going to have to look after this ¹.................... .
Class 3B - they never, ever behave ²....................! Some examples of the kids in the class. Anthea Gibbons is a nice girl but she spends the whole day looking at ³.................... in the mirror in her bag. Paul Stephens is a little mad - he spends most of his time talking to ⁴.................... in the back row. Andrew Right and Paul Rizzi fight with each other all the time and make lots of noise. If I'm very lucky maybe they'll hurt ⁵.................... and have to go to hospital. (Heh, heh, heh! No, I mustn't think things like that, must I?)
Every day I ask ⁶.................... the same question - why don't I get another job? Then I tell ⁷.................... that at least teachers get nice long holidays. And the summer holidays start in 2 weeks' time! I'm going to take the family to Wales where we can all really enjoy ⁸.................... going for nice long walks in the mountains. I hope the children don't fall over and hurt ⁹.................... though! And I hope that the dog behaves ¹⁰.................... and doesn't start chasing sheep! Oh, so many things to worry about!

Indefinite pronouns

You form indefinite pronouns with **some-**, **every-**, **any-**, **no-**:
some- and **every-** with positive meaning,
no- with negative meaning but positive verbs,
any- with negative verbs.

Add **one** or **body** to talk about an unspecified person.
There is **someone** at the door.   **No one** enjoyed the party.

Add **thing** to talk about an unspecified thing.
It was too dark. I could**n't** see **anything**.

Add **where** to talk about an unspecified place.
The kids left a mess **everywhere**.

1 Write the words in the correct places.

something
everyone
anyone
anywhere
someone
nothing

1 .... had a lovely time. We were all happy!
2 Mum, we're hungry, can we have .... to eat?
3 Has .... seen my pet snake?
4 Don't be afraid. There is .... scary in the attic.
5 I can't find my schoolbag ....
6 Oh, ... loves me!

2 Match the sentences in **1** to the pictures.

3 Match the two parts of the sentences.

1 Mum, we've seen **someone**
2 Is there **anyone** here
3 There was **nothing** to
4 There's **nowhere** we
5 I want **something** special
6 Is there **anywhere**

a worry about.
b stealing your car!
c can go for our picnic.
d who understands French?
e I can put my gold fish bowl?
f for my birthday.

4 Put the words in the correct order.

1 in / left / lessons. / schoolbag / the / Somebody / after / classroom / a

2 that / were / told / ill. / Nobody / you / me

3 café. / at / something / eat / can / we / the / Perhaps

4 for / Have / got / birthday? / you / mum's / anything

5 need / got / have / the / We / for / everything / beach. / we

6 during / didn't / I / the / anybody / exam. / to / talk

5 Look at the two pictures and write sentences.

1 something   Fiona .... (lose)
2 anywhere   She .... (can't find)
3 nobody   At home .... (can help)
4 somewhere Her mobile .... (ring)
5 everyone   She finds it! .... (be happy)

6 Complete the dialogue.

something (x4)
anything
everyone
nowhere
somewhere

Rob I'm bored, Jeff. Can you suggest ¹................................. we can do?
Jeff What would you like to do, Rob?
Rob I'd like to do ²................................. interesting, but I'm not sure what.
Jeff Why don't we build ³................................. with our new Meccano set?
Rob No, I don't want to do ⁴................................. as difficult as Meccano.
Jeff Let's go ⁵................................. to play football.
Rob It's raining, there's ⁶................................. we can go. And it's too tiring.
Jeff Really, Rob, ⁷................................. knows that you only like watching TV!
Rob Well, there is always ⁸................................. I like in the afternoon.

First Conditional

Hello! See me on the CD-ROM to discover more about *first conditional* and to learn better when to use it.

You use the 1st conditional when there is a real possibility that the situation or action in the *if* clause will happen in the future.

If you **break** a mirror, you**'ll have** bad luck for seven years.
If it**'s** sunny tomorrow, we**'ll have** a picnic.
The teacher **will be** angry if you **don't do** the homework.
We **won't go** to London at the weekend if my dad **has to** work on Saturday.

1 Match the beginnings and endings of the sentences.

1 If we go to London,
2 You won't win
3 If we miss the bus,
4 No one will come to the party
5 If I play really well tomorrow,
6 I won't do well in the test
7 If you eat a lot just before you go to bed,
8 We won't go out tomorrow

a you won't sleep well.
b if the weather isn't nice.
c I'll get a souvenir T-shirt for you.
d if you don't tell them about it soon.
e if I don't study tonight.
f if you don't play as well as you can.
g we'll get a taxi.
h I think I'll win the game.

2 Match the sentences and the pictures.

1 If you don't turn it down, I'll call the police.
2 If you leave that there, someone will get hurt.
3 If you stay there too long, you'll get sunburn.
4 If you walk on that, you'll fall in.
5 Your feet will get cold if you don't wear these.
6 If you play with those, you'll burn your fingers.
7 If I hurry, I'll get there before it leaves.
8 If I don't hurry, I won't finish before the end.

3 Complete the sentences using the phrases in the box.

Box: I lend / I'll lend / I buy / I'll buy / I watch / I'll watch / I don't go / I won't go

1 If I get some money for my birthday, ... a new MP4-player.
2 If it rains tomorrow, ... to the match.
3 I won't have any money left if .... those shoes.
4 .... TV tonight if there are some good programmes on.
5 If you haven't got enough money, ... you £20.00.
6 I think Jim will be really angry with me if .... to his party.
7 I'm so tired! If .... any more TV, I'll fall asleep!
8 If .... you £20.00, will you give it back to me tomorrow?

4 Underline the correct options.

1 If *we leave* / *we'll leave* now, *we get* / *we'll get* there before 2 o'clock.
2 *I go* / *I'll go* out tonight if the teacher *doesn't give* / *won't give* us any homework.
3 *You don't* / *You won't* finish your work if *you keep* / *you'll keep* on playing computer games.
4 If *you do* / *you'll do* that again, *I'm not* / *I won't be* friends with you anymore.
5 I think *she's* / *she'll be* happy if *you ask* / *you'll ask* her to go to the movies with you.

5 Match the sentences from 4 with the pictures.

6 Put the words in the correct order.

1 get / we'll / on time. / we / If / there / hurry,
   If we hurry, we'll get there on time.
2 it / wet. / rains, / you'll / If / get
   ....
3 a big party. / I / the competition, / win / I'll / have / If
   ....
4 come, / bus / the / walk home. / If / we'll / doesn't
   ....
5 we'll / we / late. / leave now, / If / be / don't
   ....
6 if / my camera. / angry / I'll / you / break / be
   ....
7 be fun / don't / The party / if / come. / won't / you
   ....
8 you / a coat. / don't / if / You'll / cold / wear / be
   ....

7 Look at the pictures and complete the sentences. Use the verbs in brackets to help you.

1 If she .... (cycle) too fast, ... (fall off).
2 If it .... (rain), ... (get wet).
3 If you .... (eat) too quickly, ... (feel ill).
4 If you .... (drink) this, ... (feel better).
5 If he .... (break) the window, ... (go off).
6 If we .... (make) a noise, ... (fly away).
7 If we .... (not make) a noise, ... (not see) us.
8 If I .... (not play) better, ... (not win).

8 Make the sentences. Join the ideas using *If* ….

1 Alex + get money for his birthday → he / buy a new bike
   If Alex gets money for his birthday, he'll buy a new bike.

2 we + score a goal now → we / win the match

3 people + not stop using cars → smog / get worse

4 I + not finish my work → I / not get good marks

5 the weather + not get better → our plane / not take off

6 computer + be very expensive → I / not buy it

7 the film + not be good → I / leave in the middle

8 you + not save your work → you / lose it

And now go to the CD-ROM and do the **Cartoon for Fun!**

Present perfect with *for* / *since*

> Hello! See me on the CD-ROM to discover more about *present perfect with for / since* and to learn better when to use it.

You use the *present perfect* to talk about actions or situations which began in the past and that are still in some way true now.

I have lived here since 2002 (= I started to live here in 2002, and I still live here.)

Form: Subject + **present form of** *have* + **past participle of the verb**.

You use *for* to show the length of time between when the action started and now.

I've lived here **for twelve years** / **for a long time**.

You use *since* to refer to the point in time when the action or situation began.

since 2006; since Christmas; since my last birthday; since I got your phone call.

1 Complete the crossword with the past participles of the words in the box.

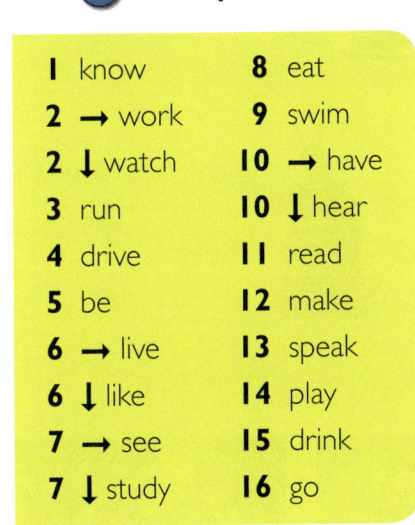

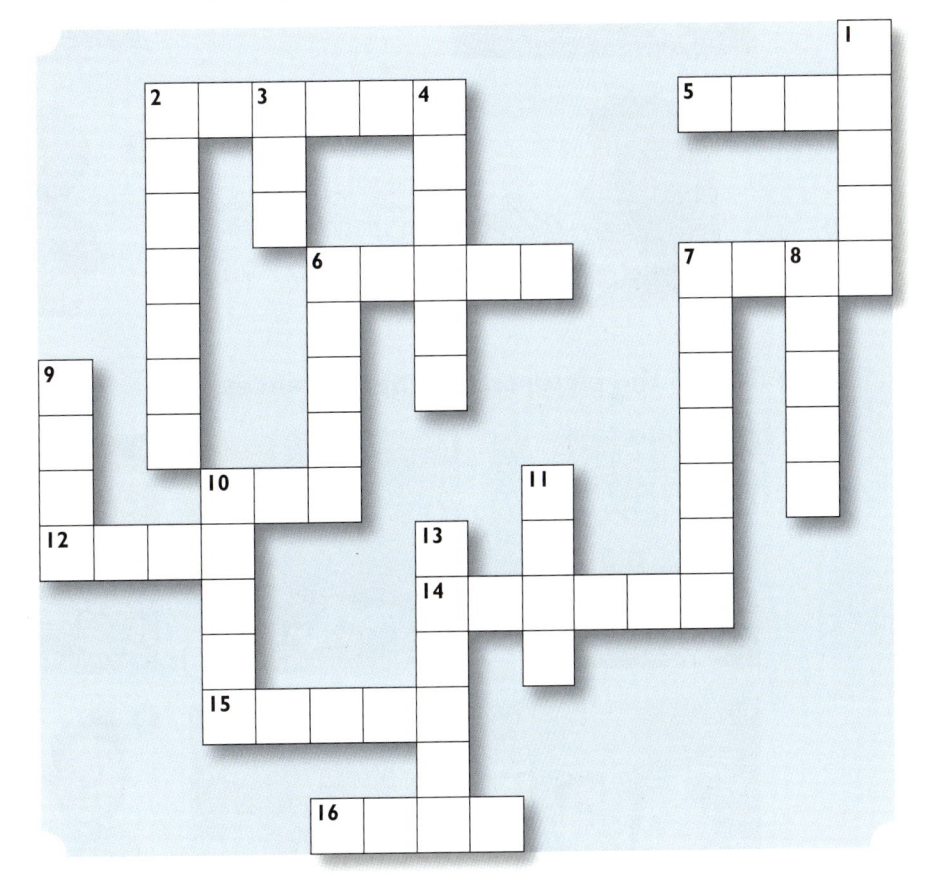

1 know	8 eat
2 → work	9 swim
2 ↓ watch	10 → have
3 run	10 ↓ hear
4 drive	11 read
5 be	12 make
6 → live	13 speak
6 ↓ like	14 play
7 → see	15 drink
7 ↓ study	16 go

2 Underline the correct word.

1 I've *lost / lose* my school bag.
2 She's *ate / eaten / eat* everything.
3 We've *win / won* first prize!
4 He hasn't *do / did / done* his homework.
5 You haven't *drunk / drink / drank* any water.
6 I haven't *make / made* a kite before.
7 Have you *forgot / forgotten / forget* my name?
8 Have they *spent / spend* all their money?

39

3 Write the past participles of the verbs from the box in the sentences.

fall
buy
make
~~go~~
wash
cut
break
see

1. They've ....been.... to a football match.
2. Fido's .... the vase.
3. He's .... out of the tree.
4. She's .... her finger.
5. She's .... a new hat.
6. What's the matter? Have you .... a ghost?
7. Oh no. Dad's .... dinner tonight.
8. Lucy! You haven't .... the dishes.

4 Match the pictures and the sentences.

1. We've only had the dog for a week.
2. She hasn't been to school since Monday.
3. I've been here for hours!
4. They've lived there for 80 years.
5. They haven't spoken since 1998.
6. He's only worked here since this morning.
7. I've known him since we were little boys.
8. He hasn't drunk anything since yesterday.

5 Match the questions and answers.

How long have you known Tim?
How long have you liked Lady Gaga?
How long have you worked in the shop?
How long have you had that bike?
How long have you studied English?
How long have you been here?

Since the 3rd year of school.
For 6 months. It's my first job.
For about three years. He's my best friend.
For hours. Where have you been?
Since last year. She's my favourite singer.
Since my birthday last Monday.

6 Choose the correct words.

Sue What's the matter, Donna? You look terrible.
Donna I feel terrible. I've got a test in two hours. I'm really worried.
Sue Have you studied?
Donna Studied! I haven't done anything but study [1] *for / since* the last two weeks.
I haven't slept [2] *for / since* days.
I haven't watched TV [3] *for / since* Tuesday.
I haven't been on the Internet [4] *for / since* Wednesday.
I haven't eaten [5] *for / since* about 48 hours.
I haven't been out of the house [6] *for / since* the weekend.
I haven't played any music [7] *for / since* years.
I haven't even spoken to my best friend [8] *for / since* this morning!
Sue So do you want to come shopping with me?
Donna Yes. That's a great idea.

7 Complete the sentences about you.

1 I haven't slept for ....
2 I haven't watched TV since ....
3 I haven't been on the internet for ....
4 I haven't eaten since ....
5 I haven't been to the cinema for ....
6 I haven't spoken to my best friend since ....
7 I haven't been shopping for ....
8 I haven't read a book since ....

8 Write the phrases in the correct column.

a few seconds
yesterday
July
an hour ago
three months
more than an hour
1987
days
a long time
Monday

for	since

41

9 **Write *for* or *since*.**

My family have lived in Chester ¹.................. twenty years but we've only had this house ².................. 2004. My dad's a journalist. He's worked at the local paper ³.................. more than ten years now. He loves his job. My mum's a doctor but she hasn't worked ⁴.................. April because she has to look after my baby brother. He's only six months old. I go to St Thomas' Primary school. I've studied there ⁵.................. three years now. I like it. It's a good school. The headmaster, Mr Newson, has been there ⁶.................. ages. I think he must be about 100. Next year I'll go to Bishop's High school. My sister's there. She's only been there ⁷.................. nine months. She's says it's terrible. I just think she wants to scare me. My best friend is called Jim. I've known him ⁸.................. the first year at school and we've been best friends ⁹.................. a long time. He's great. We do everything together. We both play in a local football team. He's played for it ¹⁰.................. last September but I've only played for it ¹¹.................. about two months. He's a bit better than me but I don't care. I just love playing football.

10 **Complete the spaces (..........) with the *present perfect* form of the verb in brackets and the spaces (_____) with *for* or *since*.**

Tim Hello professor. I ¹.................. you _____ ages. (not see)

Prof Well I ².................. out of the house _____ April. (not be)

Tim Why not?

Prof I ³.................. busy _____ the last three weeks. (be)

Tim Busy?

Prof Yes, I ⁴.................. a time machine. (make)

Tim A time machine. Does it work?

Prof Yes. I ⁵.................. it three times. It works perfectly. (test)

Tim Can I have a go?

Prof Sure. ⁶.................. you .... in a time machine before? (travel)

Tim Not ⁷_____ about a year.

Prof OK, when do you want to go back to?

Tim Um. What about three minutes ago?

Prof OK. Get in, sit down and push the red button.

(*whizz, bizz, clink, clank, whirrrrr, bong, bang, whizz*)

Tim Hello professor. I ⁸.................. you _____ ages. (not see)

And now go to the CD-ROM and do the **Cartoon for Fun!**

Past simple and Present perfect

> Hello! See me on the CD-ROM to discover more about *past simple and present perfect* and to learn better when to use them.

Past simple

You use the *past simple* to talk about actions and situations that you see as completely in the past. With the *past simple*, you often use time expressions that are about certain points in the past: **last Monday / last week / last month**; a week ago / a year ago etc.

> Last night I **watched** a film on TV but I **didn't enjoy** it very much.
>
> We **didn't go** to Italy last year – we **went** in 2010.
>
> When **did** you **start** going to school?
>
> **Did** they **have** a good time at the party last weekend?

Present perfect

You use the *present perfect* to talk or ask about actions and situations that happened in the past, but you are not interested in <u>when</u> they happened. With the *present perfect*, you often use words like: **ever, never, always, just**.

> I'**ve just watched** the new Adam Sandler film.
>
> We'**ve been** to Italy lots of times.
>
> **Have** you **started** your homework yet?
>
> I'**ve always enjoyed** parties at Patsy's house.

1 Read the pairs of sentences. If the first sentence is true, do we know that the second sentence, in brackets, is also true? Write *Yes* or *Don't know*.

1. My father bought a car. (He still has the car.) — *Don't know.*
2. My father has bought a car. (He still has the car.) — *Yes.*
3. Graham has gone to Italy. (He is still in Italy.) — ....
4. Graham went to Italy. (He is still in Italy.) — ....
5. She went to bed. (She is still in bed.) — ....
6. She has gone to bed. (She is still in bed.) — ....
7. He grew a beard. (He still has a beard). — ....
8. He has grown a beard. (He still has a beard). — ....

2 Look at the underlined verbs. Which tense is each one? Write **PS** (*past simple*) or **PP** (*present perfect*) in the brackets.

1. **A** Have you finished (..*PP*..) that book yet?
   B Yes – I took (..*PS*..) it back to the school library yesterday.
2. **A** I bought (..........) a present for Molly yesterday – you know it's her birthday on Tuesday.
   B I know, but I forgot (..........). I haven't bought (..........) anything for her yet.
3. **A** Have you done (..........) the homework yet?
   B No, not yet. But I've finished (..........) my project.
   A Me too. I gave (..........) my project to Mrs Harris yesterday.
4. **A** I've got really bad toothache.
   B Oh, that's a shame. How long have you had (..........) it?
   A It started (..........) this morning.
5. **A** I wrote (..........) loads of emails last night.
   B Did you send (..........) me one?
   A No, sorry.
   B Shame. I haven't had (..........) any emails for a long time.
6. **A** So – here you are! You've finally arrived (..........)!
   B Sorry I'm late. The bus didn't come (..........). How long have you been (..........) here?
   A I got (..........) here an hour ago, Graham!

3 Underline the correct options (I = Interviewer, M = Melissa).

A job interview

I So, Melissa — your job at the moment is with Spick Computers.
M That's right — I'm a programmer there.
I And how long ¹ *did you work / have you worked* there?
M Well, ² *I joined / I've joined* Spick in 2009. So — let me see — ³ *I worked / I've worked* for them for about two years now.
I Good. And before that?
M Before that, ⁴ *I was / I've been* a student. But ⁵ *I took / I've taken* a year off after university. ⁶ *I worked / I've worked* in France, and then ⁷ *I travelled / I've travelled* for seven months.
I Really? How long ⁸ *did you stay / have you stayed* in France?
M About four months.
I And ⁹ *was that / has that been* your first time in France?
M Oh no. I think, since I was a kid, ¹⁰ *I went / I've been* to France about ten times. My parents go there every year!
I Do you speak French?
M A little. ¹¹ *I learned / I've learned* some French at school, of course. But since then ¹² *I forgot / I've forgotten* a lot!
I Sure. OK. Well, thank you. We'll call you next week, OK?
M Fine. Thanks a lot.

4 Put the verbs in brackets into the correct tense — *past simple* or *present perfect*.

A Mike Jean's a good friend of mine.
Terry How long ¹ ...*have*... you ...*known*... (know) her?
Mike Oh, for about four years.
Terry Really? So long? Where ² .... you .... (meet) her?

B Sandy ³ .... you ever .... (eat) Arabic food?
Jasmine No, never. But I ⁴ .... (eat) Turkish food.
Sandy Really? Where?
Jasmine There's a great Turkish restaurant in Kingston — we ⁵ .... (have) dinner there lots of times. In fact, we ⁶ .... (go) there last night — the food ⁷ .... (be) great!

C Marie Hi Julie — I'm looking for James. Do you know where he is?
Julie Sorry, no. I ⁸ .... (not see) him since 10 o'clock.
Marie That's a pity. I want to talk to him. He ⁹ .... (phone) me last night but I ¹⁰ .... (not be) at home.
Julie You're lucky! He ¹¹ .... (phone) me ten times since Tuesday.
Marie I don't understand.
Julie Well, last weekend, James and his girlfriend Molly ¹² .... (break) up. Then on Monday he ¹³ .... (call) me and ¹⁴ .... (ask) me to be his new girlfriend! I said No, of course. He says he ¹⁵ .... always .... (want) to go out with me. But I've heard that before!
Marie Oh I see — and now he keeps phoning you.
Julie That's right. But now I've blocked his number! He can't call me anymore!

5 Put the verbs in brackets into the correct tense – *past simple* or *present perfect*.

Hi Andy
Look, I know ¹ *I haven't written* (not write) for a long time – I'm sorry! But I ²........................ (have) so many things to do since last July, which was the last time I ³........................ (write) to you. Anyway, I've got lots of news for you. First of all, my dad ⁴........................ (find) a job in London, so we're all going to move there in two months' time. That means I have to find a new school. I ⁵........................ never .... (move) school before so this isn't going to be easy! Well, I ⁶........................ already .... (look) at a few online, and next week we're going to London to look at houses and I'll look at schools, too. The really bad thing about the move is this – last week I ⁷........................ (start) going out with a girl. Her name's Lucy and I ⁸........................ (know) her since we were at primary school together. We ⁹........................ (meet) up again at a party three weeks ago. I'm sure she really likes me. I ¹⁰........................ (not tell) her yet that we're moving to London – do you think I should?
Last week Alex ¹¹........................ (tell) me that you've got a girlfriend too. Is that right? Write and tell me about her!
Sorry, I have to go now – I'll write again soon.
Best, Paul

6 Two time expressions are correct, and one is incorrect. Cross out the one that is incorrect.

1 Your friend Jimmy called you *ten minutes ago* / ~~*just*~~ / *while you were out*.
2 I haven't had anything to eat *for three hours* / *yesterday* / *since breakfast*.
3 My parents have been married *since 2002* / *for ten years* / *in 2002*.
4 I saw that film *never* / *on Sunday* / *last weekend*.
5 I didn't sleep well *since Friday* / *last night* / *on Sunday night*.
6 We've had this car *since 2007* / *when I was a small boy* / *for a long time*.
7 I read loads of comics *when I was younger* / *when we were on holiday last year* / *since my childhood*.

7 Re-write the sentences. Use the words in brackets.

1 We've known Mr and Mrs Parker for many years. (met)
 We met Mr and Mrs Parker many years ago.

2 They got here ten minutes ago. (been)
 They ....

3 She bought her new phone yesterday. (since)
 She ....

4 Annie has just left. (five minutes)
 Annie ....

5 How long have you had that computer? (buy)
 When ....

6 The last time I had a holiday was two years ago. (haven't)
 I ....

45

8 Put the verbs in brackets into the correct tense – *past simple* or *present perfect*.

Aesop's Fables: The wolf and the dog

A wolf was walking past a rich man's house. A dog sitting outside the house ¹....saw.... (see) him and ²................ (stop) him.

'Mr Wolf – how are you?' said the dog.

'I'm not well,' said the wolf. 'I am terribly hungry. I ³................ (not eat) for almost three days. And you?'

'Oh,' said the dog. 'I ⁴................ (not be) hungry for years. I ⁵................ (have) a wonderful breakfast this morning. My master in the house here, he feeds me very well every day.'

'You are lucky, then,' said the wolf.

'Look,' said the dog. 'Why not come and live here with me? My master will be happy to have you here, I'm sure. He ⁶................ always .... (want) a wolf in his home. And he will feed you well.'

So the dog and the wolf ⁷................ (walk) round to the back of the house, and ⁸................ (go) into the garden. The wolf ⁹................ (see) a chain on the floor, with a collar at the end of it.

'What is that?' ¹⁰................ (ask) the wolf.

'Oh, that's nothing,' said the dog. 'My master puts the chain on me every night. At first I ¹¹................ (not like) it, but I ¹²................ (wear) it every night for years now, so I'm used to it.'

The wolf stopped and looked at the dog.

'Is that right? Well, I ¹³................ (be) a free animal all my life. No one ¹⁴................ ever .... (put) a chain on me – and they never will. Better hungry and free than well-fed and in chains. Goodbye.'

9 Complete these sentences so that they are true for you.

1 Last Saturday, I ....
2 Since Sunday, I ....
3 I .... for a long time.
4 I .... two years ago.
5 .... last weekend.
6 .... for more than a year.

10 Complete the sentences. Use the *present simple*, *present perfect* and *past simple* forms of the verb.

walk

I ¹ ...walk... to school every day. I ² .... to school since I was a little girl. Yesterday I got to school late because I ³ .... too slowly!

work

My mum ⁴ .... in a bank. She ⁵ .... there for five years. Before that, she ⁶ .... in a shop.

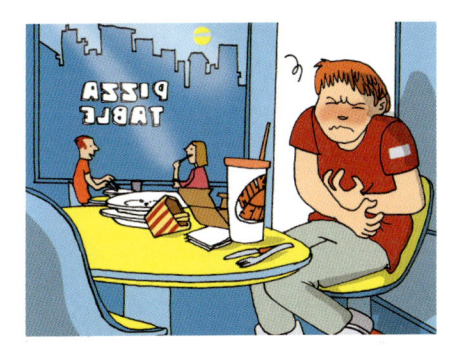

eat

Last night we went to 'Pizza Table'. I ⁷ .... two pizzas and a milk shake. I always ⁸ .... too much when I go to a pizza place. And right now I don't feel well, either – I think I ⁹ .... too much again!

play

My cousin ¹⁰ .... tennis for the first time when he was six years old. Now he ¹¹ .... tennis professionally – he's really, really good! Since 2010, he ¹² .... in more than twelve competitions – but unfortunately he's never won one.

And now go to the CD-ROM and do the *Cartoon for Fun!*

Present perfect continuous

Hello! See me on the CD-ROM to discover more about *present perfect continuous* and to learn better when to use it.

You use the *present perfect continuous* to talk about an activity that started in the past and still continues now, and to focus on how long an activity has been in progress.

Form: Subject + **has/have** + **been** + *-ing* form of the verb.

How long **have** you **been living** in California?
We**'ve been living** here for more than a year.
Since I came here, I**'ve been learning** Spanish.
We**'ve been exploring** California.
He **hasn't been here** since last Tuesday.

1 Match the pictures and the sentences.

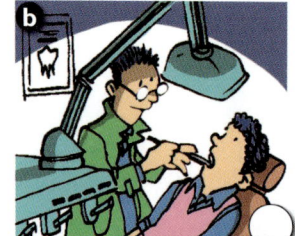

1 How long has it been hurting you?
2 How long have you been queuing?
3 They've been arguing for half an hour.
4 I'm sorry. I haven't been listening to anything you said.
5 Wake up. You've been sleeping all morning.
6 He's been doing it for ten hours now. He's trying to break the world record.
7 She hasn't been taking lessons for very long.
8 I've been working here for sixty years.

2 Underline the correct word.

1 I've been learning French *for* / *since* 4 years.
2 They've been travelling around Europe *for* / *since* August.
3 We've been waiting to talk to him *for* / *since* 10 o'clock.
4 She's been trying to phone him *for* / *since* hours.
5 My dad's been painting the house *for* / *since* 5 weeks now.
6 You've been asking me that question *for* / *since* days!
7 The dog hasn't been feeling well *for* / *since* Tuesday.
8 He hasn't been speaking to me *for* / *since* the party.

3 Complete with *for* or *since*.

Dear Mum and Dad,
We've been travelling around Italy ¹................ two months now and we've been having a brilliant time. We're in Rome at the moment. We've been staying with some friends ²................ a few weeks now and I think we're going to stay here for a while. I've also been having Italian lessons - two hours every day ³................ last Friday! I'd like to get a job here so I need to improve my Italian quickly. The weather's not been great. It's been raining ⁴................ four days and I haven't been out of the flat ⁵................ the weekend. I hope you are both well and haven't been missing me too much ⁶................ I left.
I miss you both.
Love,
Anne

4 Complete the poem with the words in the box.

haven't been listening
've been thinking
's been calling
been eating
haven't been getting
's been getting
's been sending
haven't been

He ¹................................ me every day
and every night at ten.
I ²................................ any rest
Now that Ben's in love again.

'I ³................................ sleeping well'
He tells me this and then
he says I ⁴................................
And that he's in love again.

'I haven't ⁵................................ much.
It's all because of Jen
I ⁶................................ about her all the time'
It's true. Ben's in love again.

He ⁷................................ texts night and day.
I need a new best friend.
Yes, life ⁸................................ very busy
Because Ben's in love again.

49

5 Complete the dialogue with the *present perfect continuous* form of the verbs in brackets.

DJ That was 'Dream Away' by the *Lost Boys* – a record I haven't played for a few weeks now. And I'm joined by Mike Dread, singer of the *Lost Boys*, on the telephone. Mike how are you and what ¹.................... you and the band .... (do)?

Mike Hi Zoe, and thanks for playing the record. Well, we ².. (live) in Jamaica for the last six months.

DJ Jamaica. Wow!

Mike Yes. We ³.. (record) songs for a new CD, which we hope to release next month.

DJ Well that's great news. What's the new CD like? Are there any surprises?

Mike Dave, our drummer, ⁴.. (learn) the guitar so he plays guitar on some songs but the rest isn't too different to the last one.

DJ And will we be seeing the band playing any shows soon?

Mike Well, we ⁵.. (practise) the new songs but we're not quite ready to play them live yet.

DJ I hope you ⁶.. (not work) too hard.

Mike No. It's not been all hard work. We ⁷.. (have) a lot of fun too. I ⁸.. (take) having surf lessons, for example. It's been a great six months. A lot of fun.

6 Use the verbs in the box in the *present perfect continuous* to complete the sentences.

sleep
grow
look
sleep
wait
kiss
look
sit

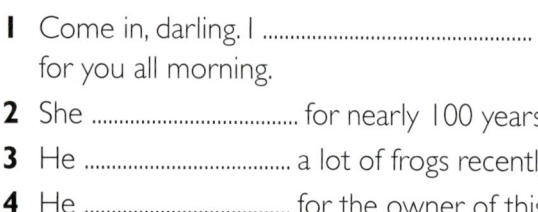

1 Come in, darling. I .... for you all morning.
2 She .... for nearly 100 years.
3 He .... a lot of frogs recently.
4 He .... for the owner of this slipper for a week now.
5 Who .... on my bed?
6 How long .... your hair?
7 Thank you. I .... in that lamp for years.
8 You .... at yourself all morning.

7 Look at the pictures and write sentences. Use the *present perfect continuous*.

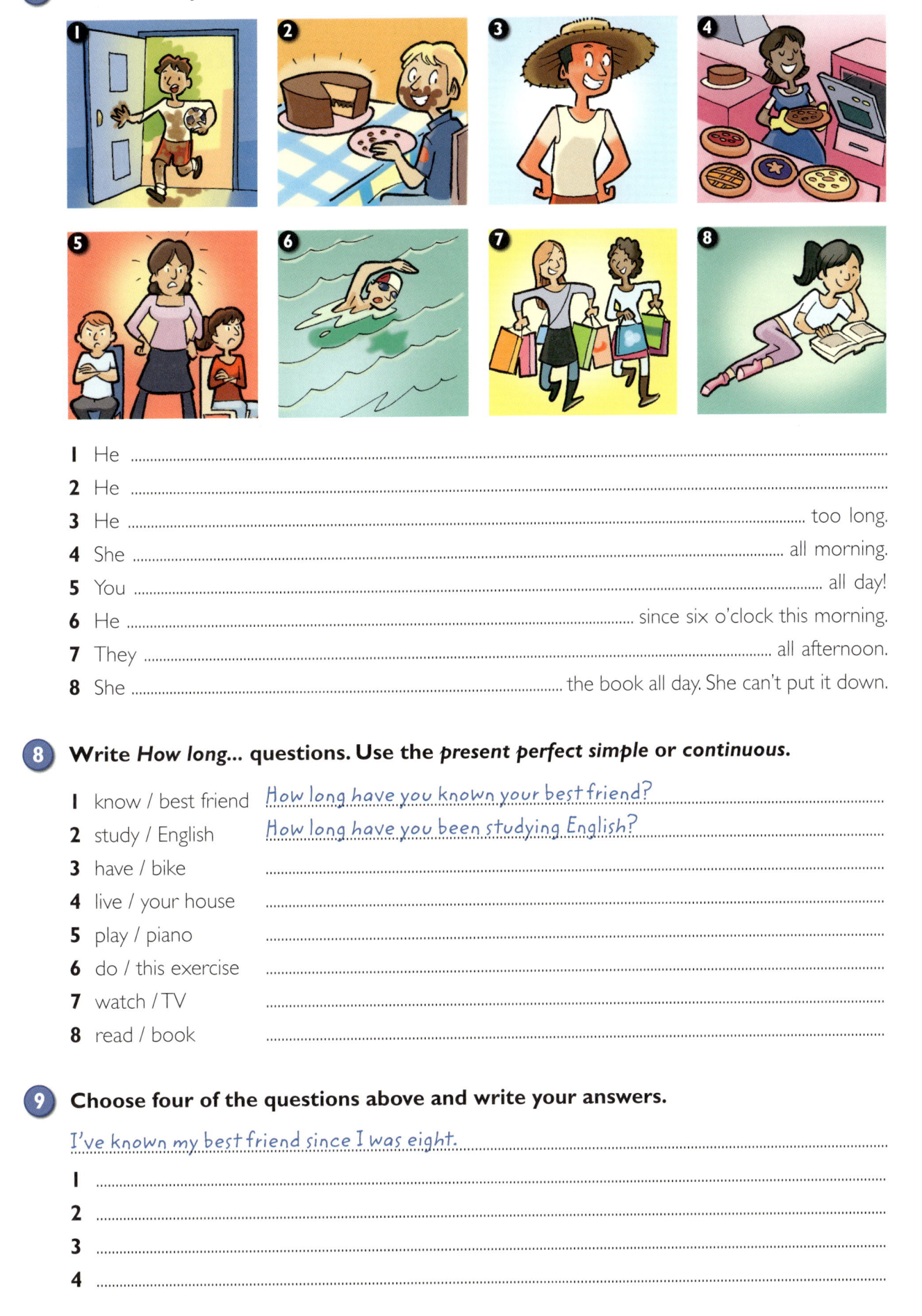

1 He ....
2 He ....
3 He .... too long.
4 She .... all morning.
5 You .... all day!
6 He .... since six o'clock this morning.
7 They .... all afternoon.
8 She .... the book all day. She can't put it down.

8 Write *How long...* questions. Use the *present perfect simple* or *continuous*.

1 know / best friend   *How long have you known your best friend?*
2 study / English   *How long have you been studying English?*
3 have / bike   ....
4 live / your house   ....
5 play / piano   ....
6 do / this exercise   ....
7 watch / TV   ....
8 read / book   ....

9 Choose four of the questions above and write your answers.

I've known my best friend since I was eight.

1 ....
2 ....
3 ....
4 ....

Put the verbs in brackets into the correct tense. Use the *present perfect continuous* or the *past simple*.

1

A How long .... you .... (wait)?
B For about two hours.
A Wow. So when .... you .... (get) here?
B At 10 o'clock.

2

A How long .... Shelia .... (go out) with Dan?
B For about two months.
A So how .... it .... (start)?
B At her party, I think.

3

A How long .... they .... (live) next door to you?
B Since April.
A And where .... they .... (live) before?
B Australia, I think.

4

A How long .... he .... (cry)?
B For a very long time.
A What .... he .... (do)?
B He .... (fall) off his bike and .... (cut) his knee.

5

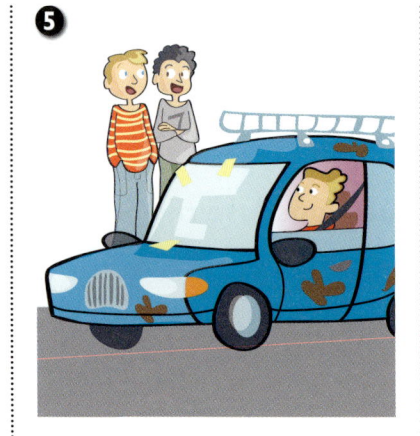

A How long .... your brother .... (drive) that car?
B He's had it since Monday.
A Where .... he .... (get) it from?
B Dad .... (buy) it for him for his 18th birthday.

6

A How long .... you .... (walk)?
B Hours.
A What time .... you .... (start)?
B Five o'clock this morning.

And now go to the CD-ROM and do the Cartoon for Fun!

be allowed to

Hello! See me on the CD-ROM to discover more about *be allowed to* and to learn better when to use it.

You use **be (not) allowed to** to talk about things that other people say you can (not) do.

My brothers and I **are allowed to play** in the street because there isn't a lot of traffic.
I**'m not allowed to go out** when it's dark – my parents say it's too dangerous.

1 Complete the sentences with the words in the box.

feed the animals
skateboard
eat picnics
cross the road
play football
stand up
make a noise
pick the flowers

1 You aren't allowed to .... here.
2 You aren't allowed to .... here.
3 You aren't allowed to .... here.
4 You aren't allowed to ....
5 You aren't allowed to .... here.
6 You aren't allowed to .... here.
7 You aren't allowed to ....
8 You aren't allowed to ....

2 Complete with *allowed* or *not allowed*.

Beth It's not fair. I'm ¹ *not allowed* to do anything.
Dad What do you mean?
Beth Well, Jim's ²............................... to do everything. But I've got to follow all your rules.
Dad For example?
Beth Well, Jim's ³............................... to go out all night. I'm only ⁴............................... out until 10 p.m.
Dad But …
Beth And Jim's ⁵............................... to buy CDs and he's ⁶............................... to listen to them loud. But I'm not. I'm .... even .... to use your stereo.
Dad Well …
Beth And I'm ⁷............................... to buy my own clothes. But Jim's ⁸............................... to wear what he wants.
Dad Yes Beth but …
Beth And Jim is ⁹............................... to see his friends whenever he wants. I'm only ¹⁰............................... to see my friends on Saturday.
Dad Yes Beth, but it's different with Jim.
Beth What dad? Why's Jim so special?
Dad Well Jim is twenty Beth.
Beth So?
Dad And you're only eight.
Beth You always say that. It's just not fair!

53

3 Put the verbs in brackets into the correct form.

Saturday morning

1 We 're allowed to stay in bed late if we want to. (stay ✓)
2 If we wake up early we .... into the living room on our own. (go ✓)
3 We .... on the TV. (turn ✓)
4 But we .... it up loud. (turn ✗)
5 Kevin .... us anything we want for breakfast. (make ✓)
6 But he .... the oven. (use ✗)
7 I .... with my toys. (play ✓)
8 But I .... on the piano. (play ✗)
9 We .... anything we want as long as it's quiet. (do ✓)

Because the number 1 rule on Saturday mornings is:

10 We .... up our mum and dad. (wake ✗)

4 Write the sentences (✓ = allowed, ✗ = not allowed).

1 I ✓ walk home from school / ✗ cycle
   I'm allowed to walk home from school but I'm not allowed to cycle.

2 Jim ✓ go out at the weekend / ✗ go out during the week
   ....

3 The children ✓ play in the park / ✗ play in the street
   ....

4 The dog ✓ sleep on the sofa / ✗ to sleep on my bed
   ....

5 My sisters ✓ wear jewellery / ✗ wear make up
   ....

6 You ✓ listen to me / ✗ talk
   ....

7 We ✓ have yogurt / ✗ have ice cream
   ....

8 Lucy ✓ go to my party / ✗ stay very late
   ....

5 Complete with one word in each space.

Kim's Bedroom — Do not come in!

You are not .... enter if I'm not in my room.

.... not allowed to sit on my bed.

.... to borrow CDs (but you must bring them back).

.... to make a mess.

.... draw in my books.

.... are .... to use my computer (if you ask me first).

You .... not .... to read my diary.

.... are .... eat sweets (as long as you give me some).

6 Write the rules for your bedroom.

.... Bedroom — Do <u>not</u> come in!

You ....
You ....
You ....
You ....
You ....
You ....
You ....
You ....

And now go to the CD-ROM and do the **Cartoon for Fun!**

could / couldn't (ability)

> Hello! See me on the CD-ROM to discover more about *could / couldn't* and to learn better when to use them.

You use **could** and **couldn't** to talk about ability in the past (**could / couldn't** are the past forms of **can / can't**).

When Sarah was a little girl, she **could walk** on her hands.
(an ability in the past that was generally true – positive)

When Timmy was a little boy, he **couldn't tie** his shoelaces.
(an ability in the past that was generally true – negative)

Our dog ran away yesterday – I **couldn't catch** it.
(an ability at one point in the past – negative)

If you want to talk about an ability (positive) at one point in the past, use **was / were able to** (not **could**).

Our dog ran away yesterday but I **was able to catch** it.
(NOT: ... but I could catch it)

The homework last night was difficult – I **couldn't finish** it.

The homework last night was easy – I **was able to finish** it.
(NOT: ... I could finish it.)

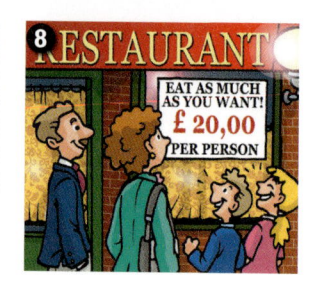

1 Complete using phrases from the box.

could climb
couldn't climb
could play
couldn't play
could eat
couldn't eat
could see
couldn't see

1 It rained a lot on Sunday so we .... tennis.
2 They gave me some food but it was horrible – I .... it.
3 When she was young, she .... the tallest tree in the garden.
4 The person in front of us at the cinema was so tall, we .... the screen!
5 Alan tried really hard but he .... the wall.
6 In the last summer holidays, there was lots of sunshine so we .... tennis almost every day!
7 When I was a small boy, I .... mountains from my bedroom window.
8 We found a great restaurant on our holidays last year – we .... as much as we wanted!

2 Complete each sentence. Use *could* or *couldn't*.

1 My sister ...*could*... walk when she was only 10 months old.
2 I knew the answers to eight of the questions, but I .... answer the last two.
3 They were talking very loudly – I .... hear everything they said!
4 I tried very hard but I .... eat everything – I left some food.
5 My granddad says that when he was a boy, he .... walk twenty metres on his hands.
6 They invited us to the party but we .... go.
7 He speaks French well now – but when he first went to France, he .... speak a word!
8 Mum looked everywhere for the keys but she .... find them. So we .... use the car – we had to walk to school!

3 Underline the correct options.

Their problems didn't stop them

Many famous people in the past had problems – but the problems didn't stop them, and they became very good in what they wanted to do. Here are some examples.

The famous German composer **Ludwig von Beethoven** started going deaf when he was about 30 – he ¹*could / couldn't* hear the music that he wrote. But he ²*could / couldn't* still write music and conduct orchestras.

When she was a little girl, **Wilma Rudolph** ³*could / couldn't* walk very well because she had polio. But in 1960, she won three Olympic gold medals for running.

Leonardo da Vinci was an Italian painter. He ⁴*could / couldn't* read or write very well – but he painted wonderful pictures and invented incredible machines.

Joseph Conrad, who was Polish, went to England when he was 23, and at first he ⁵*could / couldn't* speak English – but later in his life he wrote many stories in English and became a very famous writer.

4 Complete with *could* or *couldn't* and the verb.

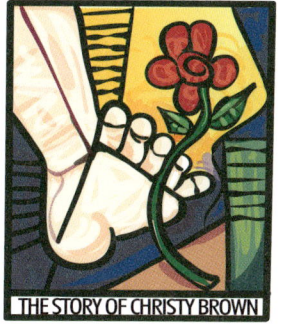

Christy Brown was born in 1932 in Ireland. He had a disease called cerebral palsy – he ¹...*couldn't talk*... (✗ talk) and he ²................. (✗ move) well. Doctors told his parents to give up. But his parents were sure that Christy ³................. (✓ think), and they talked to him all the time, although he ⁴................. (✗ answer).

Then one day Christy used his foot to take a piece of chalk and made a mark on the floor with it. Soon his family saw that Christy ⁵................. (✓ write) – using his foot! He learned to spell, and after a few years he ⁶................. (✓ read) too.

Christy wrote a book called *My Left Foot* when he was 22. He died in 1981, but in 1989 a film was made of his book. In the film, people ⁷................. (✓ see) what an amazing person Christy was.

And now go to the CD-ROM and do the **Cartoon for Fun!**

be able to

Hello! See me on the CD-ROM to discover more about *be able to* and to learn better when to use it.

You use **was(n't) / were(n't) able to** to say that, at a certain moment in the past, someone had / didn't have the ability to do something.

We **were able to** get tickets for the show.
I **wasn't able to** answer all the questions before the exam ended.

You also use **be able to** when it isn't possible to use **can** or **could**, for example when you form the future or the present perfect.

I'm very busy next weekend, so I **won't be able to come** to your party.
He had a bad accident last year, and since then he **hasn't been able to walk** properly.

Form: Future: **will / won't be able to** + base form of the verb.
Present perfect: **have(n't) / has(n't) been able to** + base form of the verb.

1 Underline the correct words.

1. We *will / won't* be able to see it better when the cloud moves.

2. We *were / weren't* able to eat it all so we brought some home for you.

3. I *was / wasn't* able to catch the last train so I'll be home soon.

4. They *could / couldn't* hear the bird but they couldn't see it.

5. I *have / haven't* been able to find the problem and it's not as serious as I thought it was.

6. She *could / couldn't* find a parking space anywhere so she left it on the pavement.

7. You *will / won't* be able to walk on it for two weeks.

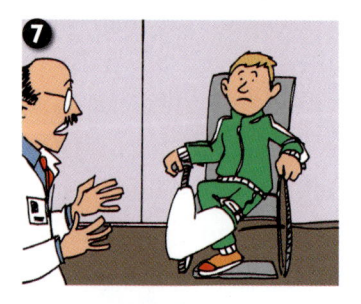

8. She *has / hasn't* been able to eat anything for a day now.

2 Match the sentence halves.

1 It was such a scary film that
2 If it snows again tomorrow
3 I had so much homework last night
4 If I save all my pocket money for six months
5 The weather's been really good so
6 There weren't many people on the plane so
7 He spoke so fast
8 The view from the mountain was great and

a I'll be able to buy a new bike.
b we were able to have two seats each.
c I haven't been able to sleep for weeks.
d I couldn't understand a word he said.
e we've been able to do a lot of work in the garden.
f we won't be able to go on the school trip.
g we could see for miles.
h I wasn't able to finish it all.

3 Read and underline the correct option.

What a terrible party. I've been here for two hours and I still ¹ *wasn't / haven't been* able to speak with Katie Pimm. The problem is that Wayne Tranter. He's been with her all night and no one else ² *has been / was* able to get anywhere near her. I don't even think she wants to be with him. She just ³ *can't / couldn't* get away. And of course, he's got a car so he ⁴ *will be / has been* able to give her a lift home. I came on my bike. I don't think she'll want a lift on that. Look at them laughing. How horrible. That's a picture I ⁵ *wasn't / won't be* able to get out of my head for days. I wanted to invite her to come to the party with me but I ⁶ *wasn't / haven't been* able to speak to her at school today. Guess why? That guy Tranter was with her all day. I tried to find her alone for a minute but I ⁷ *couldn't / can't*. Oh well. It's probably a good idea if I go home now. None of my friends are here and I ⁸ *haven't been / wasn't* able to meet anyone new. What a terrible idea it was to come here anyway. But just a second. What's this? Wayne Tranter is putting on his coat and leaving. Katie's looking at me. Is she smiling? I think she is. Maybe I ⁹ *have been / will be* able to have some fun at this party after all!

4 Complete the sentences with the phrases in the box.

to tidy up
to give away
to find our way
to fly
to get
to play

1 The baby cried all night and no one was able .... any sleep.
2 One day we will all be able ....
3 I haven't been able .... my room yet.
4 We were able .... to the top because we had a map.
5 We haven't been able .... all the dogs yet.
6 He won't be able .... football for a month.

5 Complete with *haven't, won't, wasn't* or *will / 'll*.

Tricia Have you bought the plane tickets yet?

Martin Not yet.

Tricia Well if you don't do it soon, we ¹........................ be able to get the cheap ones.

Martin The problem is that my computer isn't working. I ²........................ been able to get online for two days now.

Tricia Have you looked in the manual? There's a problem check list in it.

Martin I spent three hours looking for it last night but I ³........................ able to find it anywhere.

Tricia Well, phone Dave. He's really good at computers. He ⁴........................ be able to fix it for you.

Martin I tried him twice this morning but I ⁵........................ able to get through to him.

Tricia That's strange. It sounds like we've got a problem with our phone line. I'm going to check.

Martin I've already had a look but I ⁶........................ able to find anything wrong with it.

Tricia Hmm. There's something wrong here.

Martin Where?

Tricia I think I know why you ⁷........................ been able to do anything on the phone. Look here at the phone plug.

Martin What's wrong with it?

Tricia What's wrong with it? Well, it's supposed to be in the wall like this. Look. Now you ⁸........................ be able to do everything!

6 Complete the sentences with the correct form of *be able to*.

1 I ate too much dinner last night and I .... fall asleep for hours.
2 Ask mum. She knows everything. I'm sure she .... help you.
3 We've got a problem with our water and I .... have a hot bath for four days!
4 It was so dark we .... see anything.
5 I passed my test last week. I .... drive since Friday.
6 It was a good thing we had our phone with us so we .... call for help.
7 Do you know where Rob is? I .... speak to him for days now.
8 I'm sorry but we're going away this weekend so I .... go your party.

And now go to the CD-ROM and do the **Cartoon for Fun!**

can't be / must be

To express certainty:
use **must (be)** when you are almost sure that something is true.
use **can't (be)** when you are almost sure something is NOT true.

To express possibility or probability:
use **might/may (be)** if there is a real possibility that something is true.
use **could (be)** if there is a vague possibility that something is true.

They travel in a private jet. They **must be** rich.	=	99% sure
Everybody is going to school. It **can't be** a holiday.	=	99% sure
I didn't see him at school. He **might/may be** ill.	=	70% sure
Are we playing in the final? We **could be** on TV.	=	50% sure

1 Complete the sentences with *can't be* or *must be*.

1 People are on the beach in their swimsuits. It .... hot.
2 The pavements are dry.
   It .... raining.
3 The leaves are falling off the trees.
   It .... autumn.
4 Nobody is at work today.
   It .... a holiday.
5 The children don't want any lunch.
   They .... hungry.
6 You don't want to take your exam?!
   You .... serious.

2 Match the sentences in 1 to the pictures.

3 Choose the correct option.

1 Tom has had a huge hamburger. He *can't be / may be* hungry.
2 He has finished his homework. He *might be / can't be* tired.
3 Somebody is at the door. It *might be / can't be* dad, he is at work.
4 She knows everything about cells. She *must be / can't be* interested in biology.
5 I haven't seen my neighbour for a week. He *can't be / could be* on holiday.
6 The restaurant is always full. It *can't be / must be* a good one.
7 They are wearing lots of jumpers. They *must be / can't be* cold.
8 There are lots of people at the bus stop. The bus *may be / can't be* late.

Present simple passive / Past simple passive

You use the passive
- to talk about things that happen / happened to people
- to talk about how things are / were done
- when it's not important who does / did the action

Form: Person / thing + **be** + **past participle** of the verb.

Present simple passive

Gold **is found** in South Africa.
Thousands of pizzas **are eaten** every day.

Past simple passive

This house **was built** in 1852.
We **weren't invited** to the party.

If you want to say who (or what) does / did the action, use **by**.

This blog **is written by** my friend Pauline.

If a verb has two objects, you can make the passive in two ways:

They gave me a prize → A prize was given to me.
I was given a prize.

Hello! See me on the CD-ROM to discover more about *present simple passive / past simple passive* and to learn better when to use them.

1 Complete each sentence using a phrase from the box.

plays
writes
eat
tells
kill
~~is played~~
is written
are eaten
is told
are killed

1 Basketball ....*is played*........ in hundreds of countries.
2 My uncle Mac .... really funny jokes.
3 Lions .... other, smaller animals for food.
4 My father .... an article for the local newspaper every month.
5 Hamburgers .... in restaurants all over the world.
6 Unfortunately, many people .... every day in car accidents.
7 I can't understand this — it .... in Greek.
8 My brother .... guitar in a band.
9 It's a very famous story — it .... by people in many different cultures.
10 Gorillas .... fruit and leaves.

2 Underline the correct options.

1 Every morning at school, we *sing / are sung* a song together.
2 The national anthem *sings / is sung* before big sports events.
3 I *use / am used* my computer to do all my school work.
4 Computers *use / are used* for just about everything now.
5 Millions of tons of rubbish *throw / are thrown* away every day.
6 My aunt *speaks / is spoken* English, French and Portuguese.
7 English *speaks / is spoken* here.
8 The 7.45 flight to Paris *delays / is delayed* until 8.30.

3 Put the words in the correct order.

1 in / Ferraris / made / Italy. / are
   Ferraris are made in Italy.
2 this restaurant. / is / served / Only / fresh food / in
   ....
3 day. / trees / cut down / are / of / every / Hundreds
   ....
4 by / tested / are / products / Our / robots.
   ....
5 grown / rice / Is / Brazil? / in
   ....
6 spoken / are / in / languages / How many / Switzerland?
   ....

4 Put the verbs into the correct form of the *present simple passive*.

Choosing the 'best picture'

We all know what 'The Oscars' are, don't we? That's right – the film awards that [1] *are given* (give) every year by the Academy of Motion Picture Arts and Sciences in the USA. But how are the winners chosen? This is how it works:

- Hundreds of films [2] .... (watch) by the 6,000 members of the Academy during the year.
- The members of the Academy [3] .... (ask) to name their five 'best films' of the year.
- A list of ten films [4] .... (put) together.
- The votes for each film [5] .... (count).
- The name of the winning film [6] .... (announce).
- The 'Oscar' [7] .... (present) to the director of the film.
- A speech [8] .... (give) to say 'thank you'.

5 Active or Passive? Put the verbs in brackets into the correct form.

How a book [1] *is produced* (produce):

First, a writer [2] .... (get) an idea and [3] .... (send) an example to a publishing company. The example [4] .... (read) and if the company [5] .... (like) it, the writer [6] .... (ask) to write the book. The book [7] .... (write) and then it [8] .... (send) to the publishing company*. There are people at the company called editors, and the editors [9] .... (check) the material. If they [10] .... (find) any problems, the material [11] .... (send) back to the writer, who [12] .... (change) it.
The material [13] .... (give) to the designers, who [14] .... (prepare) the pages. The pages [15] .... (check) to make sure there are no mistakes!
Finally, the book [16] .... (print) and copies of the book arrive in bookshops.

6 Complete the sentences. Use the past participle of the verbs in the box to form the passive.

break
find
see
send
shoot
speak
~~win~~
write

1 The 2010 World Cup ..was won... by Spain.
2 The world record for the 100 m race .... in 2008 by Usain Bolt.
3 John Lennon, of *The Beatles*, ... and killed in New York in 1980.
4 In 1849, gold .... in California and thousands of men went there to get it.
5 Hundreds of years ago, many different languages .... in Britain.
6 The film *Avatar* .... by more than 100 million people in 2010.
7 The man confessed to the crime and he .... to prison for 10 years.
8 *Yesterday* is a song that .... by Paul McCartney.

7 Match the two parts of the sentences and choose a verb from the centre. Then write the sentences.

1 The *Twilight* books	start	in 1492 by Columbus.
2 The 2004 tsunami in Asia	build	by Stephenie Meyer.
3 The first airplane jet engine	make	by Picasso in 1937.
4 The Titanic	hold	by Alexander Graham Bell.
5 The 2010 Olympic Games	paint	in 1912 by an iceberg.
6 The first telephone call	write	by an earthquake under the sea.
7 The picture *Guernica*	discover	in Vancouver.
8 America	sink	by Frank Whittle in 1930.

1 The 'Twilight' books were written by Stephenie Meyer.
2 ....
3 ....
4 ....
5 ....
6 ....
7 ....
8 ....

8 Correct the statements. Use the idea in brackets and the *past simple passive*.

1 ~~Bill Gates~~ started the Apple® company. (Steve Jobs)
   No – the Apple® ..company was started by Steve Jobs.
2 ~~Brunel~~ designed the Eiffel Tower. (Gustav Eiffel)
   No – the Eiffel Tower ....
3 ~~Stephenie Meyer~~ wrote the 'Harry Potter' stories. (J. K. Rowling)
   No – ....
4 ~~Brazil~~ won the 2006 World Cup. (Italy)
   No – ....
5 ~~Lee Harvey Oswald~~ shot John Lennon. (Mark Chapman)
   No – ....
6 ~~Britain~~ gave the Statue of Liberty to New York. (France)
   No – ....

9 Re-write the sentences. Use the *past simple passive*.

There was a big demonstration against the government in central London yesterday. The police were called to help control a large crowd. A number of things happened.

1 Someone threw stones.
   Stones were thrown.
2 Someone burnt a car.
   ....
3 Someone broke some windows.
   ....
4 Someone attacked a policeman.
   ....
5 Someone hit a woman with a poster.
   ....
6 Someone arrested fifteen people.
   ....
7 Someone took five people to hospital.
   ....

10 Complete the text. Use the *past simple* or the *past simple passive* of the verbs in brackets.

Katrina – the hurricane that hit New Orleans

In August 2005, the city of New Orleans in the southern United States ¹....*was hit*.... (hit) by a hurricane called Katrina. Katrina also ²........................ (hit) other parts of Louisiana, Florida and the island of Cuba.

Many people ³........................ (leave) the city before the hurricane arrived, but many other people ⁴........................ (stay) because it was impossible for them to leave.

Many of the sea-walls that ⁵........................ (design) to protect New Orleans collapsed. 80% of New Orleans ⁶........................ (flood), especially the poorer areas. Trees ⁷........................ (knock) down and houses ⁸........................ (destroy) or badly damaged.

Almost 2,000 people ⁹........................ (kill) by the hurricane or by the floods.

The 'Superdome', a famous sports stadium in New Orleans, ¹⁰........................ (use) to shelter people who ¹¹........................ (lose) their homes.

The US President at the time, George W. Bush, ¹²........................ (criticise) by many people for not doing enough to help with the damage that was caused by Katrina.

And now go to the CD-ROM and do the **Cartoon for Fun!**

Second Conditional

> Hello! See me on the CD-ROM to discover more about *second conditional* and to learn better when to use it.

You use the 2nd conditional to talk about imaginary situations or actions, and their possible results.

If clause:
If + person + **past simple**
Main clause:
Person + **would** + base form of the verb.

If you **came** early, we **would watch** the match together.

They **wouldn't speak** to me if they **knew**.

In the *If clause* you can use **I / he / she / it were** instead of **was**.

If I were you, I would forget about him.
If it were possible, I'd go on a world tour.

You can use the *past simple* after the verb **wish** to express a desire for an imaginary situation or action.

I wish **I were** very rich.
I wish **you lived** near me.

1 Match the sentences and the pictures.

1 If I had a longer neck, I would eat that last leaf.
2 If I wasn't so lazy, I would catch a zebra.
3 If I wasn't scared of water, I'd jump in and play.
4 If I could fly, I'd join them.
5 If I was brave, I'd go in and have a look around.
6 If we had a map, we wouldn't be lost.

2 Answer True or False about the animals in 1.

1 The giraffe wants the last leaf. ....
2 The zebra is lazy. ....
3 The hippo likes water. ....
4 The ostrich can fly. ....
5 The little bird wants to look inside the crocodile's mouth. ....
6 The birds are lost. ....

3 Are the sentences first or second conditionals? Write 1st or 2nd.

1 If I was a brilliant footballer, I'd love to play for Manchester United. *2nd*
2 If I get good marks at school this year, mum will buy me a new bike. ....
3 If I asked her to go to the cinema, she'd probably say 'no'. ....
4 If Dave wasn't so mean, he'd have more friends. ....
5 If you don't invite Jen to your party, she'll be really mad. ....
6 She won't help you if you don't ask. ....
7 You'd pass the test if you studied more. ....
8 She'd be really happy if you bought her that. ....

4 **Match the sentences and the pictures.**

1.
   a If I was president, I'd build more roads.
   b If I am president, I'll build more roads.

2.
   a If you touched it, it would bite.
   b If you touch it, it'll bite.

3.
   a If you eat it, you'll be ill.
   b If you ate it, you'd be ill.

4.
   a If I win, I'll be really happy.
   b If I won, I'd be really happy.

5 **Match the beginnings and ends of the sentences.**

The problems with my family:
1 If we had a car,
2 If my dad didn't snore so loudly,
3 If my sister was older than me,
4 If we had a bigger house,
5 If we didn't have a cat,
6 If mum cleaned the windows sometimes,
7 If my brother wasn't so annoying,
8 But then if my family was always perfect,

a I would get a good night's sleep sometimes.
b I wouldn't have to share a bedroom with my sister.
c I'd be able to see out of them.
d we wouldn't have to walk everywhere.
e we wouldn't fight all the time.
f it wouldn't be MY family.
g then she'd know how annoying little sisters are.
h then my bed wouldn't always be covered in cat hair.

6 Tick the correct picture for each sentence.

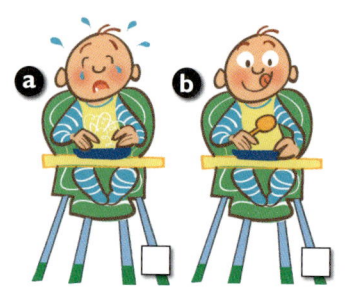

1 If the baby wasn't hungry, he wouldn't be crying.
2 If I was afraid of spiders, I wouldn't pick it up. 
3 If I had more money, I'd buy you an ice cream too. 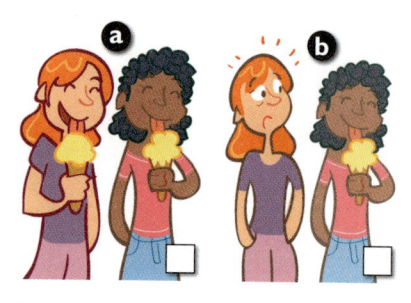
4 If we didn't have a GPS, we would be lost. 
5 If I didn't know the answer, I wouldn't put my hand up. 
6 If the sun was shining, we could go to the beach. 

7 Complete the dialogue with the missing phrases.

- wouldn't be
- had more friends
- could remember
- have more friends
- wouldn't lose things
- wouldn't ask
- knew where they were
- make such a mess

James Dave, have you seen my car keys?
Dave No. Where are they?
James If I ¹.................................... , then I wouldn't be asking you.
Dave Sorry. It's not my fault you lost them. If you were a bit more careful, then you ².................................... all the time.
James And if you didn't ³.................................... in the house, then maybe I could find things.
Dave OK. So let's think. When did you last see them?
James If I ⁴.................................... that, they wouldn't be lost.
Dave I'm just trying to help.
James Well if you just thought a bit before you opened your mouth, you ⁵.................................... such stupid questions all the time.
Dave And if you weren't so rude, you'd ⁶.................................... .
James Maybe I don't want any more friends.
Dave But if you ⁷.................................... , you'd have more people to help you find all the things you lose all the time.
James But if they were all like you, they ⁸.................................... much help anyway.
Dave I'm tired of this conversation. I'm going out.
James Where are you going?
Dave To the supermarket. Any chance of a lift?

8 Complete with the missing words.

1 What ¹.................... you do if you found a suitcase of money in the street?
  a I ².................... take it to the police station.
  b I'd ³.................... it for a while and see what happened.
  c ....

2 What would you ⁴.................... to the president of your country if you met him?
  a I ⁵.................... say anything.
  b I'd ⁶.................... him I thought all wars were a bad thing.
  c ....

3 ⁷.................... .... you do if you could turn invisible?
  a ⁸.................... creep up on my friends and scare them.
  b I'd ⁹.................... when my parents wanted me to tidy up.
  c ....

4 ¹⁰.................... .... if you saw a fight in the playground?
  a I ¹¹.................... .... anything.
  b I'd ¹².................... and stop it.
  c ....

9 Write your answers to the questions in 8 using line c.

10 Put the words in order to make sentences.

1 be / I / happy. / I'd / really / a / If / dog, / had
....

2 want / you, / number. / your / phone / she / wouldn't / If / like / she / didn't
....

3 I / If / able / be / Spanish, / to / wouldn't / Miguel. / didn't / to / talk / I / speak
....

4 at / I / better / volleyball. / I'd / short, / be / wasn't / If / so
....

5 cinema / the / to / had / I'd / money. / you / if / I / the / go / with
....

6 things. / didn't / like / best / same / if / we / all / be / wouldn't / the / friends / We
....

7 missed / bus? / the / do / school / you / What / you / if / would
....

8 choose / live / anywhere? / like / you / would / if / to / could / Where / you
....

11 Underline the correct options.

1 He would look much better if he *cut / cuts* his hair.
2 If they say anything to the teacher, we *will / would* be in trouble.
3 The police would do a better job if they *have / had* more power.
4 If she *doesn't / didn't* treat everyone so badly, she wouldn't be so unpopular.
5 I *won't / don't* tell anyone if you tell me.
6 If he *studies / studied* harder, he wouldn't get so worried about the tests.
7 If we left now, we *won't / wouldn't* have to run.
8 If she *sleeps / slept* more, she wouldn't get so tired.

12 Fill in the correct form of the verbs in brackets.

Why I'm happy being lazy …

1 If I ……*wasn't*…… (not be) so lazy, I ……………………… (do) more exercise.
2 If I ……………………… (do) more exercise, I ……………………… (not be) so bad at football.
3 If I ……………………… (play) football better, Mr Glass ……………………… (not be) so mean to me.
4 If Mr Glass ……………………… (like) me, he ……………………… (choose) me for the school team.
5 If I ……………………… (play) for the school team, I ……………………… (have to) get up early on Saturdays.
6 If I ……………………… (have to) get up early on Saturdays, I ……………………… (not be) able to go to the club on Fridays.
7 If I ……………………… (not go) to the club on Fridays, I ……………………… (not see) Jenny Ward.
8 If I ……………………… (not see) Jenny Ward, life ……………………… (not be) worth living.

13 Complete the sentences so they are true for you.

1 If I had more money ……………………………………………………………………… .
2 If I could live anywhere ……………………………………………………………………… .
3 If I could be a superhero ……………………………………………………………………… .
4 If I was older ……………………………………………………………………… .
5 If I was the President ……………………………………………………………………… .
6 If I could travel back in time ……………………………………………………………………… .
7 If I could do any job ……………………………………………………………………… .
8 If I had more time ……………………………………………………………………… .

And now go to the CD-ROM and do the **Cartoon for Fun!**

Appendix

TENSES

PRESENT TENSE

Present simple

We form the *Present simple* with the base form of the verb.
We add **-s** to the base form for the third person singular (***he*** / ***she*** / ***it***).

Affirmative	Negative	Questions	Short answers	
I **like** London.	I **don't (do not) like** London.	**Do/Don't** I **like** London?	Yes, I **do**.	No, I **don't**.
You **like** London.	You **don't (do not) like** London.	**Do/Don't** you **like** London?	Yes, you **do**.	No, you **don't**.
He **likes** London.	He **doesn't (does not) like** London.	**Does/Doesn't** he **like** London?	Yes, he **does**.	No, he **doesn't**.
She **likes** London.	She **doesn't (does not) like** London.	**Does/Doesn't** she **like** London?	Yes, she **does**.	No, she **doesn't**.
It **likes** fish.	It **doesn't (does not) like** fish.	**Does/Doesn't** it **like** fish?	Yes, it **does**.	No, it **doesn't**.
We **like** London.	We **don't (do not) like** London.	**Do/Don't** we **like** London?	Yes, we **do**.	No, we **don't**.
You **like** London.	You **don't (do not) like** London.	**Do/Don't** you **like** London?	Yes, you **do**.	No, you **don't**.
They **like** London.	They **don't (do not) like** London.	**Do/Don't** they **like** London?	Yes, they **do**.	No, they **don't**.

Present continuous

We form the *Present continuous* with ***am*** / ***is*** / ***are*** + the ***-ing*** form of the verb.

Affirmative	Negative	Questions	Short answers	
I'm (I am) playing football.	**I'm not (I am not) playing** football.	**Am** I **playing** football?	Yes, I **am**.	No, **I'm not**.
You're (You are) playing football.	You **aren't (You're not) playing** football.	**Are** you **playing** football?	Yes, you **are**.	No, you **aren't**./No, **you're not**.
He's (He is) playing football.	He **isn't (He's not) playing** football.	**Is** he **playing** football?	Yes, he **is**.	No, he **isn't**./No, **he's not**.
She's (She is) playing football.	She **isn't (She's not) playing** football.	**Is** she **playing** football?	Yes, she **is**.	No, she **isn't**./No, **she's not**.
It's (It is) raining.	It **isn't (It's not) raining**.	**Is** it **raining**?	Yes it **is**.	No, it **isn't**./No, **it's not**.
We're (We are) playing football.	We **aren't (We're not) playing** football.	**Are** we **playing** football?	Yes, we **are**.	No we **aren't**./No, we**'re not**.
You're (You are) playing football.	You **aren't (You're not) playing** football.	**Are** you **playing** football?	Yes, you **are**.	No you **aren't**./No, you**'re not**.
They're (They are) playing football.	They **aren't (They're not) playing** football.	**Are** they **playing** football?	Yes, they **are**.	No, they **aren't**./No, they**'re not**.

Present perfect

We form the *Present perfect* with ***has*** / ***have*** + the past participle of the verb.

Affirmative		Negative			Questions			Short answers	
I've (I have)		I	**haven't (have not)**		**Have**	I		Yes, I **have**.	No, I **haven't**.
You've (You have)		You				you		Yes, you **have**.	No, you **haven't**.
He's (He has)		He				he		Yes, he **has**.	No, he **hasn't**.
She's (She has)	finished.	She	**hasn't (has not)**	finished.	**Has**	she	finished?	Yes, she **has**.	No, she **hasn't**.
It's (It has)		It				it		Yes, it **has**.	No, it **hasn't**.
We've (We have)		We				we		Yes, we **have**.	No, we **haven't**.
You've (You have)		You	**haven't (have not)**		**Have**	you		Yes, you **have**.	No, you **haven't**.
They've (They have)		They				they		Yes, they **have**.	No, they **haven't**.

Present perfect + already / yet

We place **already** between **have / has** and the past participle. **Yet** goes at the end of the sentences.

| I've **already** washed the car. | We've **already** seen this film. | I **haven't done** my homework **yet**. | She **hasn't told** him **yet**. |

Present perfect + ever / never

We place **ever** and **never** between **have / has** and the past participle.

| **Have** you **ever been** to Hollywood? | I've **never been** to Hollywood. | **Has** she **ever met** a famous person? | She's **never met** a famous person. |

Present perfect + since / for

Since is used to refer to the point in time when the action or situation began.
For is used to show the length of time between when the action started and now.

| I've **been** here **since** yesterday / last week / three o'clock. | I **haven't seen** her **for** a long time / three weeks / two years. |

Present perfect continuous

The *Present perfect continuous* is formed with **has/have been** + the **-ing** form of the verb. It is generally used with **since** + point in time or **for** + length of time.

| I've **been waiting** here since eleven o'clock. | They've **been sitting** there for hours. |

PAST TENSE

Past simple – was / were

Affirmative	Negative	Questions	Short answers	
I **was** tired.	I **wasn't (was not)** tired.	**Was/Wasn't** I tired?	Yes, I **was**.	No, I **wasn't (was not)**.
You **were** tired.	You **weren't (were not)** tired.	**Were/Weren't** you tired?	Yes, you **were**.	No, you **weren't (were not)**.
He **was** nice.	He **wasn't (was not)** nice.	**Was/Wasn't** he nice?	Yes, he **was**.	No, he **wasn't (was not)**.
She **was** nice.	She **wasn't (was not)** nice.	**Was/Wasn't** she nice?	Yes, she **was**.	No, she **wasn't (was not)**.
It **was** blue.	It **wasn't (was not)** blue.	**Was/Wasn't** it blue?	Yes, it **was**.	No, it **wasn't (was not)**.
We **were** busy.	We **weren't (were not)** busy.	**Were/Weren't** we busy?	Yes, we **were**.	No, we **weren't (were not)**.
You **were** busy.	You **weren't (were not)** busy.	**Were/Weren't** you busy?	Yes, you **were**.	No, you **weren't (were not)**.
They **were** busy.	They **weren't (were not)** busy.	**Were/Weren't** they busy?	Yes, they **were**.	No, they **weren't (were not)**.

Past simple – regular verbs

We add **-ed** to the base form of the verb to form the *Past simple*.

Affirmative	Negative	Questions		Short answers			
I lik**ed** London.	I **didn't (did not) like** London.		I		I		I
You laugh**ed** a lot.	You **didn't (did not) laugh** a lot.		you		you		you
He walk**ed** home.	He **didn't (did not) walk** home.		he		he		he
She look**ed** good.	She **didn't (did not) look** good.	Did	she	like London? / rain?	Yes, she	did.	No, she	didn't.
It turn**ed** around.	It **didn't (did not) turn** around.		it		it		it
We cook**ed** dinner.	We **didn't (did not) cook** dinner.		we		we		we
You cook**ed** dinner.	You **didn't (did not) cook** dinner.		you		you		you
They lov**ed** the film.	They **didn't (did not) love** the film.		they		they		they

Irregular verbs

Present	Past simple	Past participle	Present	Past simple	Past participle	Present	Past simple	Past participle
be	was/were	been	fly	flew	flown	run	ran	run
beat	beat	beaten	forget	forgot	forgotten	say	said	said
become	became	become	hide	hid	hidden	see	saw	seen
begin	began	begun	hurt	hurt	hurt	send	sent	sent
blow	blew	blown	get	got	got	set	set	set
break	broke	broken	get up	got up	got up	shake	shook	shaken
bring	brought	brought	give	gave	given	shine	shone	shone
build	built	built	go	went	gone	shoot	shot	shot
burn	burnt (burned)	burnt (burned)	grow	grew	grown	show	showed	shown (showed)
buy	bought	bought	hang	hung	hung	sing	sang	sung
catch	caught	caught	have	had	had	sink	sank (sunk)	sunk
choose	chose	chosen	hear	heard	heard	sit	sat	sat
come	came	come	hit	hit	hit	sleep	slept	slept
cut	cut	cut	hold	held	held	smell	smelt (smelled)	smelt (smelled)
dig	dug	dug	keep	kept	kept	speak	spoke	spoken
do	did	done	know	knew	known	spend	spent	spent
draw	drew	drawn	lay	laid	laid	stand	stood	stood
dream	dreamt (dreamed)	dreamt (dreamed)	learn	learnt (learned)	learnt (learned)	steal	stole	stolen
drink	drank	drunk	leave	left	left	swim	swam	swum
drive	drove	driven	let	let	let	take off	took off	taken off
eat	ate	eaten	lie	lay	lain	take	took	taken
fall (asleep)	fell (asleep)	fallen (asleep)	lose	lost	lost	teach	taught	taught
feed	fed	fed	make	made	made	tell	told	told
feel	felt	felt	meet	met	met	think	thought	thought
fight	fought	fought	put	put	put	understand	understood	understood
find	found	found	read	read	read	wake (up)	woke (up)	woken (up)
flee	fled	fled	ride	rode	ridden	win	won	won
			ring	rang	rung	write	wrote	written

Past time expressions

We use the *Past simple* with these past time expressions.

then	ago	later	after	one day	finally	yesterday	last week	last year

Past continuous

The *Past continuous* is formed with the *past simple* of **be** + the **-ing** form of the verb.

Affirmative	Negative	Questions	Short answers	
I **was playing** football.	I **wasn't playing** football.	**Was** I **playing** football?	Yes, I **was**.	No, I **wasn't**.
You **were playing** football.	You **weren't playing** football.	**Were** you **playing** football?	Yes, you **were**.	No, you **weren't**.
He **was playing** football.	He **wasn't playing** football.	**Was** he **playing** football?	Yes, he **was**.	No, he **wasn't**.
She **was playing** football.	She **wasn't playing** football.	**Was** she **playing** football?	Yes, she **was**.	No, she **wasn't**.
It **was raining**.	It **wasn't raining**.	**Was** it **raining**?	Yes it **was**.	No, it **wasn't**.
We **were playing** football.	We **weren't playing** football.	**Were** we **playing** football?	Yes, we **were**.	No, we **weren't**.
You **were playing** football.	You **weren't playing** football.	**Were** you **playing** football?	Yes, you **were**.	No, you **weren't**.
They **were playing** football.	They **weren't playing** football.	**Were** they **playing** football?	Yes, they **were**.	No, they **weren't**.

FUTURE TENSE

(be) going to

We form the **going to**-future with **am / is / are** + **going to** + the base form of the verb.

Affirmative		Negative		Questions		Short answers
I'm	going to play football.	I'm not	going to play football.	Am I	going to play football?	Yes, I **am**. / No I'm not.
You're		You **aren't** (You're not)		Are / Aren't you		Yes, you **are**. / No, you **aren't** (you're not).
He's		He **isn't** (He's not)		Is / Isn't he		Yes, he **is**. / No, he **isn't** (he's not).
She's		She **isn't** (She's not)		Is / Isn't she		Yes, she **is**. / No, she **isn't** (she's not).
We're		We **aren't** (We're not)		Are / Aren't we		Yes, we **are**. / No, we **aren't** / we're not.
You're		You **aren't** (You're not)		Are / Aren't you		Yes, you **are**. / No, you **aren't** / you're not.
They're		They **aren't** (They're not)		Are / Aren't they		Yes, they **are**. / No, they **aren't** / they're not.

Be going to is used for future plans or intentions and when something is almost sure to happen in the future.

We're **going to** visit my uncle.	Look! It's **going to** rain.

will-future

We use the **will**-future to talk about future events and to make predictions.

Affirmative	Negative	Questions	Short answers	
I'll (I will) see you tomorrow.	I **won't (will not)** see you tomorrow.	**Will** I see you tomorrow?	Yes, I **will**.	No, I **won't (will not)**.
You'll (You will) see me tomorrow.	You **won't (will not)** see me tomorrow.	**Will** you see me tomorrow?	Yes, you **will**.	No, you **won't (will not)**.
He'll (He will) her tomorrow.	He **won't (will not)** see her tomorrow.	**Will** he see her tomorrow?	Yes, he **will**.	No, he **won't (will not)**.
She'll (She will) see him tomorrow.	She **won't (will not)** see him tomorrow.	**Will** she see him tomorrow?	Yes, she **will**.	No, she **won't (will not)**.
It'll (It will) rain tomorrow.	It **won't (will not)** rain tomorrow.	**Will** it rain tomorrow?	Yes, it **will**.	No, it **won't (will not)**.
We'll (We will) see you tomorrow.	We **won't (will not)** see you tomorrow.	**Will** we see you tomorrow?	Yes, we **will**.	No, we **won't (will not)**.
You'll (You will) see me tomorrow.	You **won't (will not)** see me tomorrow.	**Will** you see me tomorrow?	Yes, you **will**.	No, you **won't (will not)**.
They'll (They will) see you tomorrow.	They **won't (will not)** see you tomorrow.	**Will** they see you tomorrow?	Yes, they **will**.	No, they **won't (will not)**.

Present continuous for future

We use the *Present continuous* to talk about plans and arrangements already made for the future. We often add future time expressions like **tomorrow**, **next weekend**, **next week**.

What **are** you **doing** tomorrow?	I'm **going** to a concert in the afternoon.

SPECIAL VERBS

be

Affirmative	Negative	Questions	Short answers	
I'm (I am) tired.	I'm not tired.	Am I tired?	Yes, you are.	No, I'm not.
You're (You are) clever.	You aren't/You're not tired.	Are/Aren't you tired?	Yes, I am.	No, you aren't./No, you're not.
He's (He is) nice.	He isn't/He's not nice.	Is/Isn't he nice?	Yes, he is.	No, he isn't./No, he's not.
She's (She is) in class 3B.	She isn't/She's not in class 3B.	Is/Isn't she in class 3B?	Yes, she is.	No, she isn't./No, she's not.
It's (It is) blue.	It isn't/It's not blue.	Is/Isn't it blue?	Yes, it is.	No, it isn't./No, it's not.
We're (We are) busy.	We aren't/We're not busy.	Are/Aren't we busy?	Yes, we are.	No, we aren't./No, we're not.
You're (You are) busy.	You aren't/You're not busy.	Are/Aren't you busy?	Yes, you are.	No, you aren't./No, you're not.
They're (They are) twelve.	They aren't/They're not twelve.	Are/Aren't they twelve?	Yes, they are.	No, they aren't./No, they're not.

have got / haven't got

The third person singular of **have got** is (*he / she / it*) **has got**.

Affirmative	Negative	Questions	Short answers	
I've got (I have got) a dog.	I haven't got (have not got) a dog.	Have/Haven't I got a dog?	Yes, I have.	No, I haven't.
You've got (You have got) a dog.	You haven't got (have not got) a dog.	Have/Haven't you got a dog?	Yes, you have.	No, you haven't.
He's got (He has got) a dog.	He hasn't got (has not got) a dog.	Has/Hasn't he got a dog?	Yes, he has.	No, he hasn't.
She's got (She has got) a dog.	She hasn't got (has not got) a dog.	Has/Hasn't she got a dog?	Yes, she has.	No, she hasn't.
It's got (It has got) big ears.	It hasn't got (has not got) big ears.	Has/Hasn't it got big ears?	Yes, it has.	No, it hasn't.
We've got (We have got) a dog.	We haven't got (have not got) a dog.	Have/Haven't we got a dog?	Yes, we have.	No, we haven't.
You've got (You have got) a dog.	You haven't got (have not got) a dog.	Have/Haven't you got a dog?	Yes, you have.	No, you haven't.
They've got (They have got) a dog.	They haven't got (have not got) a dog.	Have/Haven't they got a dog?	Yes, they have.	No, they haven't.

there is / there are

We use **there is / there are** to say that something exists in a certain location.

There's a monster in the tree. (= There is a monster in the tree.)		There are three frogs on the table.
There was / there were (Past simple)	There has been / there have been (Present perfect)	There will be / There's going to be / There are going to be (Future)
Negative There isn't / There aren't		**Questions** Is there...? / Are there...?

Modal verbs

The main modal verbs are **should / shouldn't, have to / don't have to, might / might not, must / mustn't, can / can't, could / couldn't, will / won't, would / wouldn't, need / needn't, shall / shall not**, and **may / may not**.

I	can/can't		I	have to/don't have to	
You	must/mustn't		You		
He	should/shouldn't	come today.	He	has to/doesn't have to	go to school.
She	might/mightn't		She		
It	need/needn't		It		
We			We	have to/don't have to	
You			You		
They			They		

The forms of **be able to** are often used to replace **can** or **could**. I'm able to speak English well.

The forms of **be (not) allowed to** are used when other people say we can (not) do some things. She's not allowed to stay out late.

can / can't

Can is a modal verb and is always followed by the base form of a verb. The negative form is **cannot**, often contracted to **can't**. The past of **can / can't** is **could / couldn't**.

Affirmative	I / You / He / She / It / We / You / They **can speak** French.
Negative	I / You / He / She / It / We / You / They **can't** (**cannot**) **speak** French.
Questions	**Can / Can't** I / You / He / She / It / We / You / They speak French?
Short answers	Yes, I / You / He / She / It / We / You / They **can**. No, I / You / He / She / It / We / You / They **can't**.

can't be / must be

We use **can't (be)** when we are almost sure something is not true.
We use **must (be)** when we are almost sure that something is true.

Look at his brand new Jaguar. He **must be** rich.	The children are running about They **can't be** tired.

Note also these ways to express possibility or probability;
might / may (be) shows there is a real possibility that something is true.
could (be) shows there is a vague possibility that something is true.

Why don't you take your thick coat? It **might be** cold later.	Phone Rhyan and tell him I'm back. He **could be** worried about me.

like (doing)

We use **like doing** to say what we wish to do or enjoy doing.
The structure is: present tense of **like** + the **-ing** form of the verb.

Samantha **doesn't like reading** but she **likes listening** to music.	James **likes running** but he **doesn't like swimming**.

Conditional clauses

Conditional 1 (certain, possible)	
If clause	Main clause
Present simple	*will* / modal + base form
If it **doesn't** rain,	we'll **have** a party in the garden.
If you **feel** tired,	you **can have** a rest.

Conditional 2 (imaginary, improbable)	
If clause	Main clause
Past simple	*would(n't)* + base form of the verb
If I **won** a million euros,	I **would travel** around the world.
If you **didn't eat** so much,	you **wouldn't be** so fat.

Passive

The passive is formed with the verb **be** + the past participle of the verb.

VW cars **are made** in Germany.	Rome **wasn't built** in a day.

If a verb has two objects (e.g. My sister gave *me three books* for my birthday), the passive can be made like this:

I **was given** three books for my birthday by my sister.

We use **by** + noun to say who (or what) does / did the action.

I was chased **by** a dog.

IMPERATIVES

The imperative is equivalent to the base form of the verb (infinitive without **to**). We form the negative imperative with **do not** (**don't**) + the base form of the verb.

Run!	Don't run!
Sit down.	Don't sit down.
Open the window.	Don't open the window.

ADVERBS

We generally form adverbs by adding **-ly** to adjectives.

| usual – usual**ly** | sad – sad**ly** | furious – furious**ly** |

Adverbs of manner

Adverbs of manner show how we do something. Regular adverbs are formed by adding **-ly** to adjectives.

Regular (+ -ly) (regolare)			**Irregular** (irregolare)	
bad – bad**ly**	quiet – quiet**ly**	happy – happi**ly**	fast – fast	good – well

Adverbs of frequency (always, often, usually, sometimes, never)

0%	→	→	→	100%
never	sometimes	often	usually	always

We **sometimes** go to the cinema on Fridays.
She's **always** happy.

PRONOUNS

Question words

Who	What	Where	How often
Who is she?	**What's** your name?	**Where** are you now?	**How often** do you go to the cinema?
Who are you?	**What** eats insects?	**Where** do you live?	
Who likes ice cream?	**What** does your dog eat?		
Who do you like?			

Personal pronouns – subject and object pronouns

We have both subject and object pronouns.
We use **you**, **they** or **one** to talk about people in general.

| **Subject** | I | You | He | She | It | We | They | **Object** | me | you | him | her | it | us | them |

one – ones

We use **one** / **ones** to avoid repeating a noun.

What **book** are you reading? **One** about a man travelling around Africa.
What **kind of books** do you like? **Ones** about travel.

77

some – any

When we don't know the exact quantity of something, we use **some** in positive sentences, **any** in questions and negative sentences. We use **some** in questions when offering or requesting.

some	any	
We've got **some** cheese.	We haven't got **any** cheese.	Is there **any** milk in the fridge?
I've got **some** money.	I haven't got **any** money.	Have we got **any** strawberries?
Would you like **some** soup?	There aren't **any** onions in the kitchen.	Do you want **any** chocolate?

this / that, these / those

We use demonstrative adjectives and pronouns to talk about people or things near us (**this** / **these**) or further away (**that** / **those**).

| I like **this** jumper here. | I like **that** jumper over there. | I like **these** shoes here. | I like **those** shoes over there. |

Possessive adjectives

Possessive adjectives always precede the noun.
We do not use an article with possessive adjectives.

I	you	he	she	it	we	they
my	your	his	her	its	our	their

Possessive pronouns

We use possessive pronouns to show that something belongs to someone.

| It's **my** book. It's **mine**. | It's **his** book. It's **his**. | It's **our** book. It's **ours**. |
| It's **your** book. It's **yours**. | It's **her** book. It's **hers**. | It's **their** book. It's **theirs**. |

whose + possessive 's

We use **whose** to ask about possession.
We reply by saying the name of the person followed by **'s**.

| **Whose** is this book? | It's Amanda**'s** (book). | **Whose** book is this? | It's Rebecca**'s** (book). |

Relative clauses

Relative pronouns introduce relative clauses.

	referring to people	referring to animals or things
Subject	who or that	which or that
Object	(who) or (whom) or (that)	(which) or (that)
Possessive case	whose	whose

The pronoun can be omitted if it is the object of the relative sentence, as shown in brackets in the table.

| The man **who(m)** / **that** you met at my house is my uncle. | The car **which** / **that** we bought last month is a BMW. |
| The man you met … | The car we bought … |

Reflexive pronouns

Reflexive pronouns are used when the subject and the object of a verb are the same person. They are also used to emphasise that the subject did the action without other people's help.

| She saw **herself** in the mirror. | We did the job **ourselves**. |

| myself | yourself | himself / herself / itself | ourselves | yourselves | themselves |

Indefinite pronouns

Indefinite pronouns are used to talk about unspecified people, things or places.
For people: **some-**, **every-**, **any-**, **no-** + **one** or **body**
For things: **some-**, **every-**, **any-**, **no-** + **thing**
For places: **some-**, **every-**, **any-**, **no-** + **where**
Remember: **some-** and **every-** with positive meaning, **no-** with negative meaning but positive verbs, **any-** with negative verbs.

There's **someone** on the phone for you.
Nothing can be further from the truth.
We looked for the keys **everywhere**.
I didn't buy **anything** at the market.

PREPOSITIONS

We use prepositions in front of a noun or a pronoun to talk about direction, place or time. (see 'Time prepositions').

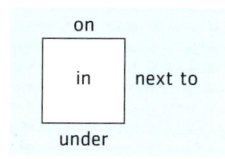

Time prepositions (*in, on, at*)

My birthday is **on** February 12th / May 28th / September 5th.
My sister's birthday is **in** December / April / June.
The film starts **at** 7 o'clock / half past eight / six forty-five.

We have Maths **in** the morning / in the afternoon.
We go to bed late **at** night.

Prepositions of place (Directions)

| at | by | behind | in | in front of | inside | near |
| next to | on | opposite | outside | over | round | under |

ADJECTIVES

as ... as

We use **as ... as** to say that two persons or things have got the same quality. We use **not as ... as** to say they haven't.

I am **as** intelligent **as** my sister.   Samantha isn**'t as tall as** Jasmine.

Comparatives & Superlatives

With one syllable adjectives we add **-er** for the comparative and **-est** for the superlative. With adjectives of more than one syllable, we form the comparative with **more** and the superlative with **most**.

My bike is bigg**er** than your bike.   My mum is **the most intelligent** person in our family.

Adjective	Comparative	Superlative
bad	worse	worst
big	bigg**er**	bigg**est**
cold	cold**er**	cold**est**
easy	easi**er**	easi**est**
fast	fast**er**	fast**est**
good	better	best
hot	hott**er**	hott**est**
long	long**er**	long**est**
new	new**er**	new**est**

Adjective	Comparative	Superlative
funny	funni**er**	funni**est**
happy	happi**er**	happi**est**
heavy	heavi**er**	heavi**est**
pretty	pretti**er**	pretti**est**
ugly	ugli**er**	ugli**est**
beautiful	**more** beautiful	**most** beautiful
boring	**more** boring	**most** boring
dangerous	**more** dangerous	**most** dangerous

CONJUNCTIONS

Linking words (and, but, because, so)

We use linking words (conjunctions) to join main clauses and dependent clauses.

> We went to the cinema **and** watched a great film.
> **but** it was closed.
> **because** we had free tickets.
> **so** we missed your call.

So (do/have) I / Neither (do/have) I

If we agree with a positive statement we say **So do I**.
If we agree with a negative statement we say **Neither do I**.
With modal verbs and **have** we repeat the verb, in all other cases we use **do** / **does** / **did**.

I **like** rap. – **So do I**.	I **don't like** rock. – **Neither do I**.
I've **got** a laptop. – **So have I**.	I **haven't got** a laptop. – **Neither have I**.
I **can** play the piano. – **So can I**.	I **can't play** the piano. – **Neither can I**.
I **went** to the cinema last night. – **So did I**.	I **didn't go** to the cinema last night. – **Neither did I**.

why / because

We use **why** to ask the reason for something. We use **because** in the reply.

> **Why** did you go to the store? – **Because** I needed bread.

QUANTITY / MEASUREMENT

How much is/are...? / How many...?

We use **how much** to ask about quantity or to ask the price of something. We use **how many** to ask about the number of things.

How much ice cream do you eat every day?	**How much** are the trainers?	**How many** pets have you got?	**How many** children are there?

A lot of, not much, not many, a little, a few

a lot of + countable or uncountable nouns.

a lot of money	a lot of biscuits

not much + uncountable nouns, **not many** + countable nouns

not much fun	not many friends

a little + uncountable nouns, **a few** + countable nouns

a little salt	a few hours

80